We Lost Her

We Lost Her

Seven young siblings' emotional and spiritual real-life
grief journey after their mother's tragic death

Ellen Krohne

Copyright 2017 by Ellen Krohne

This story is true. Quotations and remarks are adapted from memories and actual conversations and represented in the manner portrayed by those telling the story.

All rights reserved. This book or any portion thereof may not be reproduced or used in any manner whatsoever without the express written permission of the publisher except for the use of brief quotations in a book review.

Printed by CreateSpace

ISBN 9781975686734
ISBN 197568673X

Dedication

To my siblings, Dan, Tom, Bill, Betty, Annie and Gary. They bravely bared their hearts and shared their secrets in the hope of helping others in their grief journey.

In loving memory of Delores Mueller, 1930 - 1970

Contents

Acknowledgements · ix
A Word to the Reader · xi

Part 1	A Family Tragedy ·	1
Chapter 1	Growing up ·	3
Chapter 2	New Baby on the Way ·	14
Chapter 3	We Lost Her ·	21
Chapter 4	We Bury Her ·	31
Chapter 5	We Go On ·	43
Chapter 6	Back to "Normal" ·	48
Chapter 7	It Gets Worse ·	53
Chapter 8	Saving ·	60
Chapter 9	Healing ·	65
	Mom ·	73
	Photographic Interlude ·	75
Part 2	The Siblings Speak, Dad's Final Chapter and Grief Learnings ·	83
Chapter 10	Dan ·	85
Chapter 11	Tom ·	92
Chapter 12	Bill ·	103
Chapter 13	Betty ·	118

Chapter 14	Ann	126
Chapter 15	Gary	142
Chapter 16	Dad's Gone	152
Chapter 17	Learnings	167

	Appendix A Sibling Interview Questionnaire	175
	Appendix B Resources for Grievers	179
	Appendix C A Helpful Reading List	181
	Author Biography	183

Acknowledgements

Heartfelt thanks to my husband Bill. I relived my grief as I wrote, and I know there were times I was so sad he wished I'd just give up on this project. Instead he stood by me as he always has, and gave me the strength to complete it.

I so appreciate Diana Cuddeback, Director at Heartlinks Grief Center, a program of Family Hospice of Southern Illinois, for her encouragement and assistance, and for always being there for me and for those grieving in our region – she does such hard work so graciously.

Words cannot express my gratitude to my content editor, Brad Stetson; this book is much more organized, focused and of better quality because of his help. Thank you to Janet Roberts at Centering Corporation for the perfect cover design and also for her guidance and encouragement throughout this process. Thank you so much to Kathy Mueller for her excellent copy editing and Denise Keller for her expert proofreading services. Cork Tree Creative is awesome for donating their assistance with social media and public relations.

Thanks to all those, especially my Book Angels, Bill, Donna, Dorothy, Jeff and Joy, who read my drafts and gave me their blessings and encouragement.

I'll be forever grateful to my siblings, Gary, Annie, Betty, Bill, Tom and Dan, for sharing their journeys and helping me voice them in *We Lost Her*. They each shared their most intimate feelings and the story of their grief with me and you, dear reader, in this book. I love them all for that.

A Word to the Reader

My daughter-in-law, Crystal, and I were taking one of those long walks that makes a discussion about hard topics flow easily. We were discussing living a life without regrets. She asked me, "Well, Mom, if you died tonight, is there anything you'd regret?"

I answered quickly, "That I hadn't written Mom's book."

I'd retired early from my role as the Executive Director of a not-for-profit organization at age 59, for several reasons: my husband's health, wanting to move back home, to have more time with our grandchildren, to travel, and to have time to write the story of my Mother's death and the way the seven of us siblings dealt with our grief and were impacted by her loss. I've had her book in my mind and on my heart for years. I'd been retired for six months already when Crys and I took that walk. I'd taken a class on writing a book and read several books on writing a book. I just had not written a word.

So, not wanting that regret to endure, I started the next day. I've written many business documents and articles over my career, and I enjoy writing poetry. But I had never written a book.

I wrote *We Lost Her* for three reasons. First, to honor my mom. We lost her so suddenly, so unexpectedly, I wanted to put the story of our family down for the generations ahead. A story that would help them to understand the tragedy that changed us forever.

Second, if telling our story can help anyone who is grieving, or questioning their faith, that will make this worth the effort. We seven siblings each dealt with our grief in different ways. No journey was the same. I didn't intend to write a spiritual book, but faith is a big part of many of our stories. The seven of us survived and, ultimately, thrived. I am so grateful for that blessing and hope this story can help others who are grieving. I want them to trust it will get better.

The third reason for this book is to help raise funds for Heartlinks Grief Center, a not-for-profit organization that counsels grieving children and parents and offers grief services to the people in the Southwestern Illinois area. I started volunteering there about five years ago. When we realized I wasn't good at helping with grief groups (the leaders are not supposed to cry) I offered to help with their organizational development, a type of work I'd done for years as a consultant. Family Hospice of Southern Illinois, which graciously supports and is the parent organization of Heartlinks Grief Center, invited me to join their board of directors last year and I am proud to serve on it.

Half of all profits from sales of this book will go to fund the important work carried out by Heartlinks Grief Center. You can learn more about Heartlinks Grief Center at www.myheartlinks.com.

This book is structured as follows:

In Part I, A Family Tragedy, I introduce you to my family and our life on the farm. I narrate my mother's passing, her funeral and the trauma we all experienced those first few days, relating my grief journey throughout these nine chapters.

Next there is a photographic interlude which separates the two parts so you can picture all of us growing up, at the time of her death, and now. Some of the older photos are grainy and unclear, but they are the best we have. There is also a poem I wrote for my Mom several years ago.

In Part II, The Siblings Speak, I tell my four brothers' and two sisters' stories of their grief and growing up, one at a time, youngest to oldest. To enable me to voice their stories, I developed 35 interview questions, met with them and spent many hours talking, crying and laughing, and then I wrote their stories based on these discussions. (The questionnaire I used is included in Appendix A). Before each of their chapters is a short poem about their grief experience that I wrote for them. Chapter Sixteen tells the story of our Dad's death and our journey together as we lost him.

I was shocked at how much I learned from the interviews with my siblings. We lived in the same house when we lost her, but each has different, diverse, sometimes contradictory memories from the experience. I learned so much about my dear brothers' and sisters' journeys through grief and how they were impacted. I thought I knew them all very well, but I understand now that I didn't. I am grateful for this knowledge and feel closer now than I ever have to them.

The final chapter in Part II, Learnings, offers insights from our grief journeys, providing some conclusions and thoughts on managing grief. I hope these will be helpful to you.

This book is written in an informal, conversational style, using sentence fragments as a way of giving you a sense of the direct way our family communicated, in that time, in rural Southern Illinois.

I am humbled to have learned so much, and thank you for the blessing of your time to know our story, dear reader.

Part 1

A Family Tragedy

In Part One, I introduce you to my family and our life on the farm. I narrate my mother's passing, her funeral and the trauma we all experienced those first few days, relating my grief journey and the impact on my life along these nine chapters.

Chapter 1

Growing up

1970 started out as a year of change. I started high school that year and felt I may be able to leave behind my "poor kid" status I'd carried in St. Libory Grade School – like a "do-over." Hardly anyone knew me in Okawville High School. Anything and anybody I wanted to be, that's what I could be. I'd already changed my name. I could not have imagined how much else would change that year.

I was born Barbara Ellen Mueller. There was another Mueller family in town who had children with the same name as several of the children in our family. They had a Barbara Ann Mueller the same age as me. My older sister was Ann and they had a younger Ann. So, when I got to seventh grade or so, Mom decided it was all too confusing and they started calling me Ellen in school. It stuck. I liked it better than Barbie, which sounded more juvenile, in my "wanting-to-be-an-adult" 14-year-old mind.

Maybe I could even be popular in high school. I sure was not that in grade school. Even by the standards of the '60s in the small town near our farm, St. Libory, Illinois, I was not cool. I was a good girl, and a good student who longed for a change and a chance to be one of the cool kids. I know this is odd, but I really like change. I've always been comfortable with changes in my life. Maybe it was all the changes in our home as our family grew, or maybe I'm just wired that way. Little did I know how much change was ahead; change for me and my brothers and sisters - everything, our entire life.

1970: It was the start of a wild, decadent decade in the USA. The Vietnam War was raging, "free love" was the mantra and Jimmy Hendrix died of a drug overdose. Not much of these mini revolutions impacted the rural area in Southern Illinois where we grew up. Our house was remote, at the dead end of a long, very rural road three miles outside of St. Libory, Illinois, in southwestern Illinois. It is a wholesome, hardworking community where neighbors take care of each other. Just an hour from St. Louis, Missouri but a world of difference away.

Ours was a small farm that got smaller every few years, as Dad gradually sold our family farm ground to make ends meet. Even as a child, it didn't make sense to me to sell the land and think we could ever make ends meet the next year. The "Tony Mueller School of Finance" was sometimes not sensible. Dad thought and did and said things sometimes that didn't make sense to me.

Like his theory on genetics, which was all about birth order. The oldest son, Gary, had the most genes; the second son, Bill had the next most; Tom, the third son, had even less; and poor Dan, the youngest son, got what little was left. And girls, well, "Girls don't have genes," Dad said. So, the girls of the family, Ann, Betty and I, just didn't have any genetic makeup according to the world of Dad. No proof to the contrary swayed his belief in this theory; he was right and the rest of the world was wrong. That's how it was with Dad.

Don't get me wrong; he had wonderful qualities, too, my Dad. He was kind-hearted and honest, and he worked very hard to provide for us. He dropped out of school after the 8th grade, as that year his father died of diabetes at the age of 43, and Dad needed to help his mother raise his five sisters on their small farm. He sure was dedicated to his mother. We were lucky she lived just a field away with what was to happen during that year of 1970.

Dad was very intelligent, too, in spite of his weird theories. He could do math in his head quicker than anyone I knew. He worked as a carpenter and farmed our ground and his mother's. He seemed to always be working, if he wasn't hunting or fishing. He sure enjoyed those pastimes.

Heck, I didn't know we were poor until I went to first grade and I heard one of the older kids saying I was one of those "poor Tony Mueller kids." I asked Mom what that meant and I remember her holding back angry tears and saying, "We are not poor, we are rich in love." We were both - poor and rich in love. Thank God we were on a farm, because with chickens, pigs, cows, and a huge garden and arbor, we had plenty to eat. We had plenty of love, too, from Mom and from Dad in his way and from the huge extended German Catholic family that claimed us.

I had over a dozen sets of aunts and uncles and dozens of first cousins, all nearby and close to us. We saw them often and loved them. Only my dad's sister, Aunt Eleanor, who was my godmother, lived what seemed far away in St. Louis, Missouri, about an hour from our farm.

Dad joined the Carpenters Union in the late '60s and that changed our lives. We had health insurance for the first time ever. We were able to go to the dentist and have Novocain, instead of just toughing out a filling. We had crossed over a threshold of some kind; even at 12 years old, I knew the family had moved from "really poor" to "just poor." It was a big step. We went from having our electricity cut off to paying our bills.

I remember when I was in first or second grade the Tri-County Electric Company lineman came to our house in his big truck. He gave us kids a ride in the bucket of his truck, high in the air over the farm. I thought that was the coolest job ever! Then he shut off our power because the bill hadn't been paid, an apologetic look on his face that I'll never forget. My Mom sat at the table and cried, so frustrated it had come to this. Years later I worked as a customer service representative for Illinois Power, the local utility company, and had to put customers on that list for disconnection of service. I didn't forget how that felt, seeing Mom's sense of desolation, of defeat, and worked hard with them to avoid it if I could.

Mom worked hard, too, seemingly all the time. She always smelled like fresh baked bread or fresh baked or cooked something. Meal-time for a family of nine, in the day before dishwashers and microwaves, was lots of work. Cash was hard to come by, so we ate as much from the land as we could. We were organic before that was a thing.

Mom had wide, deep brown eyes that seemed to be able to see right through you and behind her back, too. She was about five feet five inches tall, with short brown hair that was always in tight curls. She was what we'd call big-boned now, strong from all the hard farm work and usually tanned from being outside a lot. She was not well educated, but smart from all the books she devoured. The thing I remember about her the most was her laugh. It seemed to come from deep inside her and would erupt in boisterous guffaws. It sounded like music to me. When Mom was laughing all was good in our home. When she was mad or upset, it served you well to stay out of her way.

Like a "mother hen" would describe how she was with her children. She was fiercely protective of us and went to great lengths to be sure her flock was well cared for and fed. She would also push us hard to get out of the nest and explore the world – to "make something of ourselves" is how she framed her desire for her chicks.

Mom had grown up in a large German Catholic family. Her name was Delores Ann Schmersahl. She had three sisters and six brothers and they lived on a small farm outside of Lively Grove, Illinois. She was number seven. A few years ago, a large coal-fired power plant was built partly on what was once their farm, but back then, it was a small farm and times were hard for the family.

Mom's father, my grandfather, Gerhardt Schmersahl, had a stroke in 1954 and was in Alton Hospital for a decade before he died in 1964. I don't remember anything about him, except hearing he had a bad temper. My Mom's mother, Anna (Grandma Schmersahl to me), had diabetes and an open sore on her leg for as long as I can remember. They called it a "milk leg." She'd had a hard life raising her children during the depression while battling her illness.

It always made her happy when her grandchildren came to visit or stay with her. She had long brown hair that she wore up in a braid. One time when I was staying with her to help her clean I came into the kitchen at night and saw her with her hair down and was awestruck at how beautiful she looked in the dim light with her long, shiny hair around her shoulders. She had a leg amputated in 1969 and died shortly after that. Just a year before the summer of 1970, so she at least escaped the pain of what happened to her daughter Delores.

Mom graduated from grade school and then was sent to work to help support the family. She was hired out to a farmer, Joe Buss, whose wife was ill and who had four small children. Mom lived with them and cared for the children and the house. Years later Ruthie, one of the little girls, told me how much Mom meant to her and how she loved her for her kind care. After Joe's wife passed, my Mom's older sister, Eleanor, met Joe and they got married just a few years after my Mom and Dad did.

While working for Joe Buss, Mom met the neighbor down the road. He was nine years older than she. His name was Anthony Henry Mueller, but everyone called him Tony. He was thin and strong and had a patch of wavy brown hair and dancing blue-green eyes. They dated, or courted as they said back then, for a few months. They were married on April 17, 1950. Mom turned 20 that year in July. She was the first of the ten Schmersahl kids to marry, although she was one of the youngest.

Even as a young girl, I understood there was a strong bond, a special love between them. Dad would tickle her while she was doing the dishes, and Mom would snap her dish towel at him, playfully. I loved to listen to them late at night talking in muffled, undistinguishable tones from their bedroom, interspersed with laughter. Even when they were fighting, they still talked at night before they went to sleep.

Mom loved babies and was hoping to have the first grandchild. She didn't get that wish as her older brother Edmond had the first grandson, but soon babies would be coming quickly to Tony and Delores Mueller. She and Dad had dreams of having an "even dozen" children. Twelve, that was their magic number.

Gary was the first baby, arriving in 1953. When Gary was little, they took a trip to Kentucky Lake, one of the few places she'd see in her lifetime outside of our little town and the St. Louis region. She talked often of that trip and how exciting it was to see other areas.

Gary was quickly followed by Ann in '55, me in '56, Betty in '58, Bill in '59, Tom in '61 and Dan in '63. A flock of seven in just ten years - they were busy! We joke now that Mom and Dad obviously had no "rhythm," which was the only sanctioned option for birth control for these strong Catholics.

My Mom's sisters tell me she was happy as a new bride and mother, working hard to put together a home for her growing family. Mom and Dad first lived in the farmhouse that I later would call Grandma Mueller and Aunt Loretta's home, the original farm place. They later traded homes with Grandma Mueller and Aunt Loretta, moving to the house across the field from the original homestead. Dad had enlarged the newer home and added a bathroom and entryway to the little house that I would always know as my home.

The house was like many little farmhouses in the '50s. From the entryway, you walked into a good-sized kitchen, an "eat-in" you'd call it now. The north wall of the kitchen was lined with cabinets, lots of counterspace and a window above the double sink. It was so nice to look out of it while doing the dishes. A large table was in the middle of the room, with five chairs around three of its sides and a long bench on the fourth side where the four youngest kids sat.

The living room was the second square room on the other side of the kitchen. It had the stairway door to the upstairs along one wall and two big windows that let in the afternoon sun on the adjacent walls. Next to the stairway was the door to Mom and Dad's bedroom. It was a big room that always had a baby cradle in it and Dad's desk on the south wall. Along the west wall Mom's cedar chest was set under a window. It held all our family treasures and had that aroma of cedar that filled the air when it was opened. Dad gave it to Mom early in their marriage, and it was one of her prized possessions.

Right next to Mom and Dad's room, there was another bedroom where we all slept until I was ten years old, when Dad finally finished the upstairs bedrooms – one for the four boys and one for the three girls. The new bedrooms didn't have heat, but felt spacious and comfortable, with the wood paneled walls and ceiling. The only bathroom was between the first-floor kids' bedroom and the kitchen. Growing up, I always felt blessed to have such a nice bathroom – it had pink and black tile that Mom kept polished and spotless. Some of my cousins on my Mom's side didn't have indoor plumbing yet, so I felt grateful for ours. The house was small, but full of activity and fun.

Simple fun. Dad would take an old tarp and put it around some timbers to make a "swimming pool" for us. We ran a hose down the hill to make a slip and slide. We played so many games of hide and seek, tag, baseball, Red Rover, and all kinds of make-believe. We'd put on "shows" for Mom and Dad. On summer Sundays Dad would barbeque. We'd all get a sip of his beer, and we'd eat outside. His ribs just couldn't be beat. In the winter Dad would pull us on a homemade sled, and we'd slide around on the frozen pond.

For special occasions, it was Uncle Raymond's homemade ice cream. We'd all get our turn at the churn and our share of the sweet, creamy deliciousness. Soda was another special treat – orange, grape, red or root beer. We'd share a bottle in these special little multi-colored tin cups, which were saved just for that treat. Our family didn't take vacations or go out to eat often or do many of the things I take for granted now. We had simple fun together.

We spent lots of time fishing. Aunt Clara and Uncle Jim fished and visited with us often. Clara was Dad's younger sister, and they didn't have a child until later in life. I remember when they finally had Nancy, their only child: it was a joyous day. She was born on Grandma Mueller's birthday, October 8, 1969. I asked Uncle Jim at Christmas if I could hold the baby, and the "no way" look quickly shone in his eyes. But Aunt Clara said it would be okay if he'd sit right by me. Hovering is what we'd call it now, but he did it with such love, it was touching.

Aunt Clara knows about grief, losing Jim when Nancy was only 13 to a sudden, massive heart attack in their home. Decades later she still had a catch in her words as she told me about that day. She said, "I always thought God gave me Nancy because He knew He was going to take Jim from me so early."

Mom kept the farmstead clean and organized. Dad was more of a packrat, filling the barns with items he may need later. The place had that eclectic look that many farmsteads have – neatly mowed grass around stuff in the yard. All in all, it was warm and safe and there was room to roam and work hard and play - a great place to grow up.

In St. Libory stood the massive Catholic church and the parochial school we attended. Mom would charge our groceries at Reutter's store in St. Libory. The grocer would put a little bag of candy for us kids in with the groceries, and it was the highlight of our week to get those Tootsie Rolls. I doubt he knew the impact of his kindness on our lives.

Once, when I think I was about eight, I went with Mom to town to get the groceries. The grocer took Mom aside when she came in and said, "I'm so sorry, Delores, but I can't let you have any more until you pay down your bill." Mom looked defeated. She was mortified, looking around to see who was listening. I was afraid she would cry. She had enough money to buy sugar and that's all. I felt so embarrassed for her, and mad that she had to be humiliated and made to feel so worthless. I didn't understand money at that age, but swore I'd always have it. No matter what. I was not going to have to rely on anyone to make it for me. I was going to do that myself. Somehow.

I was proud to give Mom my paycheck when I started babysitting for a newly married neighbor when I was 12 years old. It's amazing that they let me watch an infant all day alone, but I was very responsible and certainly experienced with caring for children due to my three younger brothers, Bill, Tom and Dan.

I was the chief "three-little-boys-watcher," and Mom relied on me to keep them out of mischief. They were good at getting into it too. They dug tunnels around the yard and the pond, captured all species of insects and birds and played hard all-day long. I relished this role, as it was better than lots of others on the farm. Annie did most of the heavy lifting with Mom in the kitchen. We all did the hard chores, too, like cutting weeds out of the bean fields in the early mornings, feeding the pigs and collecting the eggs. There was always work that needed doing.

A source of conflict between Mom and Dad as long as I can remember was Dad's drinking. I never saw my Mom take a drink of alcohol. Dad drank, starting most days with a drink from the bottle he kept high up in the cabinet, next to the few fancy glasses we owned. He was functioning every day, working and doing what he needed to do. He was never a mean drunk, but an alcoholic nonetheless. The thing Mom hated was his habit of staying after work late at the taverns.

She'd send one of us kids with him whenever she could, in the hope that would keep him from staying too long. We'd beg to be the one to go with Dad, as we'd ride with him to the Venedy Elevator during harvest season and get to watch as the grain was dumped from the truck. Then on to Moose's Tavern across the street for his beer and a shot, and we'd get a soda or candy bar.

Another source of conflict was money. Mom was reliant on Dad for money, and that's mostly what they fought about. Mom would spend money on something Dad didn't think she needed, and they'd argue loudly. I hated those fights. As a child, I didn't realize that fighting is normal behavior for married couples. I just knew I wasn't going to be a screamer when I had a family.

Mom was an excellent seamstress, and she made most of our clothes. Once when she found a sale on store-bought short sets she bought matching ones for the three boys. Dad made her take them back. She wasn't allowed to make purchases without his approval.

I remember her standing up to him sometimes, though. She wore housedresses all the while I was growing up. Beautifully made, of cotton, with pleats all around and an apron that matched. Dreadful for working on a farm and especially in the cold weather. Many women were wearing pants in the '60s, but Dad didn't want her to wear them. "I wear the pants in this family," he'd say. One day she went out to drive the tractor for Dad wearing new pants she had sewn. She smiled at him and said, "Tony, I'm doing men's work, I'm wearing them." (or something to that effect). He just shook his head and smiled back. She wore pants to work outside after that.

Mom was just starting to be able to earn her own money in that year of 1970. She started cooking at the Kaskaskia Restaurant in Fayetteville, and she watched the boys I babysat in the summer. When I look back on it, I'm amazed that she could work outside the home, given her workload at home from all of us and the farm. But she finally had a paycheck, her own money. This independence made her so proud. She seemed so satisfied and happy.

Then came 1970 and that hot summer.

Chapter 2

New Baby on the Way

We never had air conditioning - just window screens and a whole-house fan. In the country the breezes helped, though. The summer of 1970 was unbearably hot. It was the worst for Mom. She started showing in the late spring.

Mom battled her weight her entire life, and was proud when, at 40, she had finally lost some over that previous winter. She wasn't thin by any means, but less round. Always amazed me she bought those Ayds diet pills that year. There were so many other things we needed. She must have used "her money" from her restaurant job. They worked and she was happy. Until she found out she was pregnant. "I can't believe this. Finally got all of you in school!" Mom said. She smiled, too, and trusted this surprise would be a blessing to our family. Dad seemed happy, even breaking down and buying an air conditioner for the kitchen to make it a little more bearable for her.

She'd had some health issues, including very bad varicose veins that had been "stripped" a couple of times over the years, when she had to be bed-ridden for months to recover. When Dan, the youngest child, was born at home seven years earlier, the babies had stopped coming for a while.

It was July 28, 1963, my seventh birthday. Dad took Mom to the hospital that morning, but they sent her home, saying it was not time for the baby to be born yet. I remember her being upset and saying, "I've had six children, and I know when I'm ready to deliver another one." She did know. Four hours later, the ambulance came out to our house, after she and Dad had delivered Dan in their bedroom. Dad had put us all down in the basement and frantically called Grandma Mueller to come and help him deliver the baby.

We heard Mom's screams and heard the baby's first cry. We were so scared. When they took her out to the ambulance Mom stopped to show us the baby. He hadn't been cleaned up, so he was just a bloody, sticky mess. We, being little kids, vowed to love him anyway, even if he was so ugly. We prayed he'd be okay. By the time Mom and Dan came home a week later, which was the norm in those days, he was gorgeous. I thought prayer could fix anything.

And that was the end of the babies, at least for seven years. In my youthful mind, I believed it was because Dad hadn't known what pain she'd endured in order to deliver a baby, as back in the day the husband was not allowed in the delivery room. Once he actually saw one delivered, the babies stopped. Or, maybe it was because they argued more in those years; that could have been it, too. Or maybe they finally found some "rhythm."

But pregnant she was at 40, in 1970. I remember my aunts talking about a "change baby." As a 14-year-old girl, I thought it was great news. I adore babies, so in my young mind, this was as much my baby as hers. I'd be her helper, and it would all be grand.

My Aunt Loretta and Grandma Mueller, who lived across the field from our farm, were always a big part of our lives. My Grandma's name was Mary, but people called her Mamie. She was petite, round, had that same twinkle in her eye that my Dad did, and a quick wit. She baked the best chocolate chip cookies, and if you were good, you got to go across the field to their house in the summer and watch her "show" with her, which was the soap opera *Days of Our Lives*. She'd always have cookies.

Aunt Loretta was Dad's youngest sister. She was born several months after her father had died from diabetes, and she lived with her mother her whole life. She was one of the few females I knew that had a full-time job outside of the home at that time. First, she worked at a factory, then as a cook at a school. She traveled, going to Colorado once, which I thought was so exciting.

She never married, which I never will understand. She was so pretty - and extremely independent. Maybe it was her level of independence, some would say stubbornness, that kept her single. When Grandma died in 1984, she grieved for years. She never left, living her entire life in the farmhouse across the field. We felt lucky to have her across that field – she was always there for us.

My sisters, Ann and Betty, and I secretly stitched 6 blocks for a baby quilt during the summer of 1970. A dying art, cross-stitch. We still do it, making quilts for the grandbabies today. Grandma and Aunt Loretta marked and quilted it in yellow fabric, good for either a boy or girl. Mom was so surprised and touched by the quilt – she loved our little surprise baby shower.

I had started my "new life" at Okawville High School that fall. We went to Okawville High School because our farm was in Washington County, just outside the St. Clair County line. Most of my St. Libory Grade School mates went to Freeburg High School in St. Clair County. It felt like heaven to get just that little bit outside, to something new.

We were good students, all seven of us. A's were expected, nothing less. And if we brought home less, we felt it. Not that avoiding a spanking was the sole motivation – we all wanted to please Mom and Dad, and getting good grades did just that. Maybe this is a peculiarly German trait, but any time we were given a job or task, we were expected to do it very well and completely - not just a half effort. I still hear their voices ringing in my ears: "Any job worth doing is worth doing well."

Mom had this vision that we would all go to college and often told us so. Not as a subject for debate, just that we were, somehow, going to go to college, and since none of us had any real athletic ability, good grades were the ticket to college.

Mom was an avid reader. She always said the most important thing to do with a child was to read to them, right away from birth and every day. I remember her face when I was in first grade, as I read to her from that *Dick and Jane Reader* for the first time. That "I'm so proud of you" smile.

We'd get to go to the Marissa Public Library each week, if we were well-behaved, to check out books. Marissa was a little town about 10 miles from our farm. It had a grocery store, dry goods store, a doctor, a dentist and that special place, the Public Library. Mom would get books each week, too, sometimes staying up all night reading. Books were her escape. She said you could go anywhere in the world and be anything you wanted with a good book.

She appreciated the arts and music, too. We'd get the cheap (or free) seats at the Muny Opera in St. Louis, and Aunt Loretta would drive us there. She could sing "Oklahoma" as well as the leading lady, I thought. Mom would sing and whistle those show tunes while she cooked.

Mom found a way for us to play instruments in the school band, too, once the opportunity was offered at St. Libory Grade School. I played the drums, Betty was fantastic on the coronet, Bill played the tuba and Tom played the trombone. Dan wasn't old enough yet in 1970, so he never got to play in the band.

It was such fun to meet new people, and I quickly made a new group of friends in high school that seemed to like me just for who I was. I had thinned out over the summer and felt better about myself. My 5'6" and 130 pounds was just about right for those days. I had long brown hair and dark brown eyes. I had learned to sew and had made myself new clothes during the summer from some of my babysitting money. Short was in, and my skirts were. I thought life was just grand. Suddenly, even boys were interested and interesting. In World History class, I saw the cutest boy ever two rows back and one over. Little did I know he'd be with me as I write this, 47 years later.

The boy that asked me out in September 1970 was a different guy, Tom. I went to the Wheat Festival, which is Okawville's annual town celebration, with him. I introduced him to Mom. He was the only boyfriend of mine she'd ever meet.

High School Freshman Orientation was a tradition that has now long been discarded. The purpose was to "torture" the new class members through silly games. Innocent fun that if missed was a big social faux pas and sure to invoke worse torture from the upper classmen.

So, when Mom let us know that she was in labor that evening of Friday, September 25, she insisted that I attend the orientation. She didn't seem quite right, not happy like I expected her to be right before the baby was born. Her eyes were sad, like she knew something was not right. I'd overheard her talking on the phone to her sister, Eleanor, saying she hadn't felt the baby moving much, but thought it was because she was getting close to delivery. I was secretly scared that there was something wrong with the baby.

Mom's brother, my Uncle Joe, was what we called in those days "mentally retarded." After Mom's mother died earlier that year, and before Mom was pregnant, Uncle Joe came to live with us. He was a little boy in a big person's body and would get angry when things didn't go his way. When he threatened Mom in one of these moods, Dad had had enough – Uncle Joe left our house and eventually went to a state home where he lived for the rest of his life. He seemed much happier there, but Mom was upset. She was so stubborn, she just didn't want him to be "put away."

Even if the baby was born like Uncle Joe, we thought, we'd love him or her, and it would be okay. I thought that was the worst that could happen.

We all went outside to see them off as Dad pulled the station wagon up to the front door to get Mom for the trip to the hospital. She hugged each of us, and I remember saying to her, "Tie up the score, Mom, bring us home a girl." (There were four boys and three girls so far.) She frowned and said that God had already decided that one.

As they drove away we went back into the house to wait for Dad to call and let us know the baby was here. We were so excited! We knew if the baby was a boy he would be named Robert Albert. My mom's younger brother Albert was to be the godfather, as Mom had a special spot for him in her heart.

The crib had been cleaned and the baby clothes and diapers brought out from storage. Everything was ready for this new joy in the family. I had been praying so hard for this baby to be here and healthy, and praying that maybe Dad would be home more and at the tavern less with a new baby in the house. Just maybe life would be like that fairy tale ending in the romance novels I'd started reading that summer.

I went to the Freshman Orientation, halfheartedly. I was also excited, as my new friends would all be there, too, and I was anxious to let them know the baby was coming that night. The games were distracting and I got engaged in them: carrying an egg in a spoon and pushing grapes across the gym floor with my nose, and other such silliness.

Unexpectedly, I felt a "jolt" - like a shock to my body and my entire being shook. It felt like when we put our hands on the big hi-line electric poles in our south field and our hair stood on end from the voltage. I shot up and looked at the clock. It was 9:00 p.m. I had an overwhelming feeling of Mom's presence, like she was calling to me. I knew something was happening with Mom or the baby, but I was not sure what. I couldn't shake the disturbing feeling that something was wrong. Maybe I was just being paranoid, I thought. After all, all of us had been born just fine, even Dan at home.

When I got home later that evening, I was surprised that Dad was not back yet. I checked to be sure that the three little boys were sleeping soundly, and they were. I worried that Dad wasn't home yet, and I was just not sure what else to do. There were no cell phones in 1970 and no way to contact him. I prayed that all would be okay in the morning and good news of our newest sibling would be here when I woke up.

Chapter 3

We Lost Her

I was woken from a sound sleep the next morning by my older sister, Ann. Her voice was shrill and panicked, not like hers at all. "We lost her. Ellen wake up. Mom's gone!" she screamed as she shook my shoulders. I opened my eyes and focused on her face, right in mine. Ann had a desperate look on her face.

I mumbled, groggily, "What are you talking about, who's gone? Go away, Ann." She knew I needed some time to wake up: why did she come so suddenly at me like that? Then, it hit me like the roof had fallen in on me. She meant Mom. Gone. Yes, of course, she was in the hospital. But Ann's tone said more.

I tore past Ann and ran down the stairs. I had to find Dad and see what was going on with Mom. I felt numb and like throwing up. And, mad. Why would Dad send Ann to tell me – why didn't he tell me himself?

Dad was at his desk, in their bedroom. He looked gray, like he wasn't even there. His eyes were bloodshot and wouldn't even look in mine. I sensed this was not the time to scream, so I knelt down by his knee. "What happened, where is Mom?"

I've always had that ability – to be calm during a storm. I may be anxious before and fall apart after, but in the "heat of the battle," I'm calm, thinking about what needs to be done and helping to get it done. This trait was to serve me well in my roles with the electric utility I'd work with for 27 years. During crises, like ice storms, calm is required. Dad's reply to my question changed the world for all of us.

"We lost her. She died." He couldn't say anything else. He just stared, unmoving, at the papers on his desk.

"The baby?"

"He died too."

Numb is a word I use a lot to describe how I felt for the next year or so. And it started with those words from Ann. "We lost her, Mom's gone."

Gone. Never coming back. Couldn't be. How could this be? God would not do that to us – we were good people. How were we going to live without Mom? She did everything here for us. Oh God. Deep breath.

I heard my voice come back calmly. "Dad, you need to tell the boys." Gary, the oldest, must have already been up and knew, or I guessed he did; I didn't see him in the room. Gary was doing the chores, I figured. He helped Dad so much with the farm, he didn't seem to ever have been a kid.

Ann was there now. Not screaming, just sitting quietly on Mom and Dad's bed. I joined her. It felt like a long time, but was probably only minutes.

I went upstairs, and it was odd as I climbed the steps. I couldn't feel – my feet felt numb, like I was not in my body. Like this was all a dream – a nightmare, but not scary, just not real.

I roused the boys like I always did, but they must have sensed something was wrong, because they got right up. Usually they played possum, and I'd have to cajole them out of their beds. I said, "Come on downstairs now. Dad has something to tell you." I think Ann must have started breakfast, because I remember there being food on the table.

Dad came into the kitchen and he very simply stated, "Mom and the baby are in heaven." The little boys stared at him. Betty was there now, too, and Gary. We were all around the table, like we had been so many times. Never without Mom, she was always there, had to be there. Dad may not have been, but Mom was. That in itself felt weird, wrong, like every day going forward was to feel. She had to be there.

The next thing Dad said made me even madder than that he had sent Ann to tell me the news. He said, "And I don't want any of you going on a hunger strike or anything like that. Eat your breakfast." Maybe someone at the hospital told him to watch for that, because I can't imagine Dad would think we'd do that. He was right, though, I was thinking of all the things I'd never do without her, and eating was up there.

And he and Gary left.

We sat and cried. And cried. Dad hadn't hugged us or said it would be all right. Or really explained what had happened. Just that they were dead. He must have gone across the field to tell his mom, Grandma Mueller and sister, our Aunt Loretta, because it wasn't long before they came over.

I'm not sure who told the other aunts and uncles, probably Grandma Mueller and Aunt Loretta. By noon, the house was full. They came with food. Lots of food. And tears. And shock. Hushed voices as the explanation was passed to each new arrival. I heard pieces – blood clot to her heart, she didn't suffer – it just hit her; the baby was stillborn, better anyway since she didn't live; the cord wrapped around his neck, he didn't have a chance.

Nothing corroborated by Dad, just these snippets of whispered conversations – and my mind was screaming "WHAT HAPPENED??" But the adults were not going to discuss this with us kids. Although I suddenly felt not like a kid at all, more like 30. And numb. And worried – what was going to happen to us without her? How were we ever going to make it?

The aunts had the three little boys under control, and I remember sneaking upstairs to the bedroom that Ann, Betty and I shared. Betty and I slept in one bed and Ann had her own bed right by the door. I curled up in a ball and did just that – bawl. Until I felt like I had to throw up.

I wouldn't do that, of course, because I have had a mental block about throwing up ever since first grade when the nun who was our teacher made me clean up my vomit in church. I told myself the whole time, I would never throw up again. I'm like that; if I decide something, then I just have to do it. So, I didn't throw up.

But I wished I could join her – just die too. It would be easier than what I saw ahead in living without Mom; how could we do that? I wanted my baby brother to hold. He could have at least lived, and we'd have him to be part of the family. He didn't even get a chance at life. Ann and I could have taken care of him. That day I started asking the question that I've been asking for a lifetime; "Why God?"

The other recurring question in my life is – "What would Mom want you to do?" That question began that day, too. Lying there alone, crying. Figuring she was in heaven. I didn't doubt that statement: she had to be. And Robert, her son, too. Figuring she was there watching already, I wanted to do what would please her – what she'd expect. So, I went back downstairs to be sure the boys were okay. Or, at least as okay as they could be.

Tom was rocking. He did that a lot. He was a bright child, very intelligent. Not as articulate as Bill, who did most of the talking for the three boys. Tom was sensitive, and when he was upset, and even sometimes when he wasn't, he'd rock - in the rocking chair, or just back and forth. And today, Tom was rocking. Danny was playing with Lincoln Logs. Just seven, he had white-blond hair and an innocence that endeared him to all. He was a darling little boy, our baby.

Downstairs, the discussion turned to the details that had to be addressed. The funeral: visitation and caskets and prayer cards and the Mass. It was tradition to have the visitation and funeral quickly back then. I heard the words, "Get it behind us," for the first of many times that day. Mom died early in the morning of the 26th, so that gave us the next evening, the 27th, for the visitation, and then the funeral could be on the 28th.

Bill's birthday. Bill is the oldest of the three little boys. Smart as a tack, too. Thoughtful. A little mischief maker, always coming up with big ideas to get the three in trouble. It would be really hard on him to have the funeral on his birthday. But no one was thinking about that. Just get it behind us.

I got to go along to the funeral home to plan the funeral. I don't remember if I asked to go or Dad asked me to go, but I felt it an honor to be included. Gary and Ann were there, too, along with Grandma and Aunt Loretta. Gary seemed to be doing most of the talking. Dad was just staring blankly ahead.

I knew Mr. Moll. He was a tall man with soft, kind eyes. When I'd been to the funeral home previously, like for my Grandma Schmersahl's funeral the year before, he'd been the one to greet you as you entered. He knew about death and what was ahead. I didn't understand why anyone would do that for a living. That day Mr. Moll was kind and patient with us. He was apologetic for our loss, like it was his fault or something.

We sure didn't have the money to afford a fine funeral, but, of course we wanted one for Mom. At least she could have that. So many things she couldn't and didn't have in life – at least we could give her that in death.

The color of the inside of the coffin was debated. Cream, or yellow. God, please not yellow. Mom always made my clothes yellow when she sewed, and it was my favorite color already. I didn't want her to be buried in it. I think the cream won, with some blue for the baby boy. It was decided he would be in the casket with her. Inside, I was screaming- please let her just be there herself. For eternity, she'd feel her failure. That is how I imagined she'd feel that the baby had died. She was like that – things were her fault. Even when they weren't.

I didn't say anything to fight Dad and the adults, and the baby was in her arms for the visitation and in her casket for the burial. Wrapped in the handmade quilt we had made her for her baby shower. Cheaper than two of everything, I heard Mr. Moll say. I heard people at the funeral home say, "Saddest thing I ever saw." It felt that way to me, too.

We got back home and another shift of family was there preparing for supper. Things felt kind of normal – with the aunts there and so much food. For a moment, I forgot what had happened and smiled at something – and felt instantly horrible. How could I smile while she was in that funeral home alone, getting ready to be buried? I was never going to smile or laugh again.

Eventually, everyone went home and it was just us. Dad was in his chair, staring blankly, like he had been all day. Not really able to function or make decisions. We let the little boys watch television. Mom didn't allow that very often. She thought most of the programs would corrupt our minds or give us bad examples and ideas. No *Three Stooges*, no *Little Rascals*, nor any science fiction. Nothing with violence other than westerns (which, upon reflection, were pretty violent). Nothing with that rock and roll music. *The Wonderful World of Disney*, Red Skelton and Carol Burnett, those were okay.

But tonight, it was on. Distraction was important; we'd had a hard day.

By the next day, word had gotten around that Mom had passed away. There were funeral cards displayed in all the little stores in the area. It was announced at morning Mass; which Dad had made us all attend. I remember having read the cards for other people at the counter of the grocery store or at the tavern. I hate to admit I had never felt bad for the people that were dealing with the death that was announced on that card.

I remember thinking about all the people that would read her card that day and hoping they felt something. Maybe shock, maybe sadness. What I worried about later (not yet on this day) was pity. I could hear the ladies at church say, "Poor Tony Mueller kids without a mother." Pity and lots of other emotions that are hard to decipher at 14 were headed my way.

I guess it was a German thing, not to want pity or hand-outs or outside help. We were proud in that little particular way – we'd get by with what we had ourselves; we didn't need anyone's help and certainly not their pity. We were Muellers (but it was pronounced Miller, Americanized when the family moved to the United States from Germany, or maybe during the war, I'm not sure). Mom and Dad instilled the importance of sticking up for each other and taking care of each other. Family came first.

Dad asked me to be sure everyone had clothes presentable to wear to the visitation and funeral. I started with the little boys. It wasn't all the best fit, but I found white shirts and black pants, and dark socks and shoes for Tom and Dan, the two youngest. Bill had no shoes that fit him, other than tennis shoes. Betty was also a problem. Mom had recently sewed her a dress that would work fine, but the only shoes she had were not dress shoes, and Ann's and my hand-me-downs didn't fit her. I had a brown plaid vest with matching skirt I'd sewn myself. I didn't have shoes that matched, although I could have made do with some black ones that didn't quite fit. Gary must have been set, too, and Dad had a black suit that he wore to all dress up occasions and the blue tie that Mom liked. Ann was okay, as Mom had made her a nice brown dress, and she'd gotten new shoes for her Homecoming dance the year before.

"Dad, we need to get some shoes. Bill, Betty and I need them." He just kind of stared at this request, like he didn't remember what he'd asked me to do that morning. It was about 11 a.m. when he finally acknowledged this need after several attempts on my part to convey it to him. He gave me $20.00 and told me to take care of it. That was a lot of money back then, and I wanted to be careful and do a good job of spending it. Especially since Dad had never given me any money to shop for clothing; this was a big exception and responsibility.

I called Aunt Loretta and she drove Ann and me to New Athens, armed with the sizes we needed. We knew New Athens had a shoe factory outlet. What we didn't count on was the store closing at noon as it was Saturday. We got there just as the store was being locked up. I blurted out, "We need shoes for our mom's funeral; you can't close!" Fortunately, they didn't. We ran down the aisles while Loretta waited with the store clerk. I found Bill some dress shoes, and Ann found Betty a pair of patent leather black flats. I found a brown and gray crocodile-looking pair of flats. They were beautiful and a little pricey, but we didn't have time to bargain hunt. We had a couple of dollars left and I felt good that we'd gotten the job done – mission accomplished.

That good feeling didn't last long. When I got home and gave Dad the change, he was mad. "You weren't supposed to spend it all," he said. The look on his face said it all – "You should not have bought something for yourself, what were you thinking?" I felt deflated. In a short period of time, I'd gone from thinking that I'd done just right to failing in his eyes.

There wasn't time to wallow in that feeling for long. I needed to get the three little boys dressed and myself, too. We had a shower in our unfinished basement. It had concrete block walls and a concrete floor. Most of the time our basement was dry and we had lots of things stored down there.

Among the things stored were rows of jars full of the goodies Mom and we girls canned each summer from the enormous garden Mom always planted. Jelly, pickles, vegetables of all sorts, and dozens of jars of ketchup. She was rightfully proud of her canning abilities. Ann is the one who's carried on that tradition

The shower was just a shower head by the water heater, next to a floor drain. It was exciting when Dad put it in a few years earlier. There was only a tub upstairs in the bathroom and never enough hot water for everyone to get fresh bathwater, so you sure didn't want to be the last one to bathe! The shower was fun for the boys. They would run through it and imagine themselves to be pirates and all kinds of animals in the rain.

On this Saturday, the 27th of September, 1970, they didn't play long. In and out, and I had their clothes laid out on Mom and Dad's bed. Dan kept asking, "Where are we going?" and, "Do I have to wear this? I want my shorts on." and other normal seven-year-old questions. Grandma had told the boys, "Your mom is in heaven," so I did too. I think they were really confused, just not understanding the concept of death and certainly not anticipating what was ahead - not just ahead for that evening or the day of the funeral, but ahead for their lives. I'm sure they didn't understand why everyone was crying and acting sort of stunned. I felt bad for all of us, but the worst for my three little boys.

I let them watch TV again, thinking that Mom would not have approved. I went upstairs to get dressed and started thinking about what was ahead that evening. I wondered if any of my new friends from high school would be there, thinking probably not. They may not even have known about it and if they did, it wasn't like a fun thing; they probably wouldn't come anyway.

I remember getting out my journal, which I had started keeping the year before. Entries in my journal always made me think through things and helped me to sort out what to do and not do. I wrote over and over Why? Why her? Why both of them? Why this family, what had we done that was so bad that you, Jesus, could do the worst thing possible to us?

The answer came as I wrote; it was all his fault. If Dad hadn't gotten her pregnant, she would still be with us, so this must be his fault. With someone to blame, I somehow felt better. Of course, it wasn't rational, but in my 14-year-old heart, it was.

We had to be at the funeral home an hour before the visitation started. Mr. Moll said it was "family viewing time." The immediate family - Dad and the seven kids and Grandma Mueller and Aunt Loretta - would go in first. We would be followed by the other aunts, uncles and cousins. Then at five p.m., it was open to the public until nine p.m. It seemed like a long time to be in the public eye.

And, so many people came.

Chapter 4

We Bury Her

If there were ever a time I felt like I was in an out-of-body experience, it was walking into that room, with my mom in a shiny, pretty oblong box. It didn't seem at all real, much less happening to me. She had on the navy dress with the white collar, the one she'd gotten for Dan's First Communion. With the weight she'd lost, she was happy to get a new store-bought dress in a smaller size. It looked so pretty on her.

First Communion was a big deal in our family, and, like most Catholics, we celebrated it like a wedding. Dan's was no exception. She must have known she was pregnant by then, in April, and I'm sure she had no idea she wouldn't see the baby she carried. Or that soon she wouldn't see any of us again.

Robert, the baby, was at her shoulder, sort of in her arms, but not entirely. He had on a white gown, like he'd have worn at his baptism. I hadn't seen him before that moment, and it hit me hard that his little life had never even started. I felt like throwing up. But, of course, I wouldn't.

Dad went in first, and we all followed. We walked up to the coffin, and it felt like a mile across the small reception room of the Moll Funeral Home. There she was, in that pretty navy dress. She had on powder and her hair was all wrong – kind of flat, not curled like she would have liked. She did not look like my mom, which made me mad; they got it wrong! She never wore makeup like that or bright lipstick. She was pretty without that, in my mind. Not that she thought she was: she didn't have a good "self-image," I think they would say now.

We just stood there looking at her. Someone started the crying – I don't remember who, but it started - softly, no loud wailing. We knew that wouldn't be acceptable. I think the word that describes what we were expected to be is "stoic." Take it. Life gives you good and bad. Take it. What doesn't kill you makes you stronger. Take it.

I remember thinking it would be better to be in there with her. Life without her was so unthinkable. Maybe I could just climb in there and she'd take me with her. That may be better than what was ahead without her.

We stood there sobbing for only a short time. In a long row, with Gary next to Dad, then Ann and Betty, and then me with the three little boys. Dad didn't move all night, it seemed; he was there by her side.

Now Dad was crying, too. He tried so hard to be that stoic German, and he wanted us to be too. That was not his real nature. He'd seen a lot of hard times after his father died when Dad was 12. His father had had diabetes, and in those days, serious complications arose quickly. Dad didn't get to go to high school. He didn't go into the service during WWII as all his friends did, because he was rejected when he enlisted, as "4F." He was the last male in the bloodline and the head of household for the family. He didn't leave his Mother after marriage, staying just across the field when he married at 30. He was a loyal son.

I wasn't thinking about how he felt in that moment, though. I was worried about me and about my siblings. How were we going to make it? And I was so mad at him, as this was all his fault, right?

Grandma Mueller and Aunt Loretta joined us after a while. Grandma Mueller always had a kind word and a laugh. Seeing her made me feel a little better. I don't remember the three little boys being hugged and consoled by Dad or Grandma or anyone. That seems odd to me now that I'm a grandmother; I'd have scooped them up and hugged them hard. They needed that badly, and it wasn't there from Dad or others.

Someone, I'm not sure who, said we had to touch Mom. That would make it more "real" for us and help us to say goodbye. I thought, "Are you kidding me? I cannot do that." She looked so cold and not like herself at all. I did not want that to be my last feeling from her. Dad did it first - softly, like I never saw him do before. He touched her cheek. We all filed by and did it. Touching her cheek, like somehow that would make this better, or us better. It didn't. It just confirmed, yes, she is really dead. And cold. And not waking up.

I lifted Robert's fingers up in mine. The baby that was mine to take care of with her. He was cold too.

It was time for the rest of the family to come to see them before the doors opened. The aunts and uncles and cousins filed in, filling the small reception room. Aunt Maryann was very close to my mom. She was younger by six years, and since she didn't have children until later, she doted on us. She spent time with us, and there was always laughter in the house when she visited. She came when Mom had her leg surgeries and helped us so much.

Mom and her sisters, the Schmersahl girls, were known for their raucous laughter. It filled the room and lit up our lives when they were together. Mom's oldest sister was a nun, Sister Benigna. She along with Aunt Maryann, Aunt Eleanor, and Mom could go on for hours, laughing over little things. They were not laughing today. Maryann was sobbing. I'd never seen her cry, other than from laughing too hard. It had to be painful for her to lose her sister and friend. Aunt Eleanor had red eyes, too.

Aunt Eleanor was, and still is, the most positive person I know. She saw a lot of sadness in her life and accepted it, seeming to grow more positive that all would be okay. I always looked up to her and tried so hard to be like her, keeping a positive spirit. As anyone who's been through a major loss knows, it is easier said than done.

Soon people were streaming in. It seemed there was a steady flow all night, with a long line wrapping around the reception room. We seven kids were to stand by Dad, and he was right by Mom's head. The three little boys got so restless, I kept taking them to the little private kitchen area and bathroom. That was okay by me; it was hard to see all these people "viewing" her. I knew most of them from church or school, and it was nice that they came to pay their respects.

All of my grade school classmates came and some of my new friends, too. But I could barely talk to them or look at them without crying. I tried to say thank you as they muttered, "I'm sorry" or "So sorry." Some of them hugging me, others just quickly walking by. It felt like I was in a dream, in slow motion, but the picture was so sharp it couldn't be real. I kept thinking I'd wake up soon.

The rosary was said at seven p.m. The room was packed, and it was stiflingly hot. We were to all sit in the front row and pray with the St. Libory Rosary Sodality women who led the prayer. Sitting down I started looking at her, lying there on that pretty satin lining, and I lost it. I started sobbing, not quietly, not stoically -loudly.

Mrs. Mueth, who had been my teacher at St. Libory Grade School and my friend Lynn's mom, came up to me. She whispered, "Come with me." I complied and followed her to the kitchen area. She held me in her lap like a little child, and we both cried. She had the same soft roundness of Mom and every bone in my body ached for this to be my mom, not my friend's mom. I'll never forget her kindness to me that night, to know I just needed some comforting. After a little while, she dried my eyes and told me to be brave, that Mom would like it if I was, right? I went back to my place, with the rosary still being prayed, and Dad shot me one of those "How could you?" looks.

There was so much food in the funeral home kitchen – cookies and cakes and sausage. The boys ate way too many cookies and were running around like it was a party. I felt bad when I yelled at them to sit down and behave. I knew they were too young to understand what was going on. I was having trouble comprehending it, no less these little ones.

People kept saying, "She's in a better place, she's in heaven now." Well, I felt like she had no business in a better place; we needed her here. There could be no better place for her to be. Here, with me, with us.

I remember vividly some of the people who came through the line. Bill and Doris Frank, who were the parents of my boyfriend of a few weeks, came. Bill was the President of the First National Bank in Okawville, where Dad banked, and he did Dad's taxes, so he knew Dad well. Mrs. Frank brought me a present – and said "I just wanted you to have something," and how sorry she was for my loss.

I opened the package when I got home. It was the most beautiful gold suede purse, with a long thin gold metal strap and fringe on the bottom. Very stylish, not like anything I owned. It was beautiful. I just couldn't bring myself to use it. It made me too sad because of the way it came to me. I treasure it to this day.

The visitation night was long, and I was so grateful we had decided to have it for just one night, not two. I don't think we'd have made it through another. At the end of the evening, Aunt Dorothy, the wife of my mother's brother, Mike, stood on a chair and took pictures of Mom in the casket. She said "Someday you will want these to remember." I thought, "No, I won't. I don't ever want to remember this night or any going forward, only the ones before she died."

We made it through that evening, and I remember we were all exhausted when we got home. The boys were sent straight to bed after teeth brushing. We didn't even read to them, which was the tradition, just sent them to sleep. Dad looked like he'd been beaten: he was so tired, he slumped as he made it to the kitchen table. But he'd held up fine, only crying when he first saw her earlier that day. Little good that stoicism did, we were all crumbled inside, only the outside crust was holding up.

The next morning, the 28th, was Bill's 11th birthday. The day we laid her in the ground.

Mom always celebrated our birthdays in fine fashion. All the aunts, uncles and cousins would be invited to the first birthday party. After that, it was just Grandmas, Aunt Loretta, and your godparents. It was always a celebration. There weren't always presents, which we didn't expect growing up, but Mom would let you pick your cake, any kind you wanted, and she'd bake it for you. You got to lick the bowl and the beaters and eat two pieces of cake if you wanted. That was special!

Mom had a very cool cake-decorating book that had a different "cut-up" cake for each month. She'd make that month's cake for you, if that's what you picked. Bill's was the schoolhouse, probably because back in the '70s school started after Labor Day. The cake had M&M's for windows and candy corn for the sidewalk. It was a beauteous thing to behold. Even though Dan and I share a birthday, we always had separate cakes. Mine was always chocolate angel food, from heaven it was so good! No more of those in my future.

Bill didn't have a schoolhouse or any cake that day. I hate that we didn't celebrate, in spite of her burial, and have always felt bad about not making him a cake.

When I went to bed on the 27th after the visitation, I felt such relief it was over. I guess I didn't account for just how hard the next day would be. My dreamlike feeling just continued, like this was not reality – I'd wake up soon and it would all be okay. This just could not be happening.

The next morning the weather was bright and sunny. A gorgeous fall day, just like Mom loved. We got up with the "Our Father" blaring from KMOX at 6 a.m., like every day. There were the normal chores to do: gather eggs, feed the animals – cows and pigs and dogs. Make breakfast and get the little boys up, fed and dressed. These things we were trained to do, and they came naturally. I remember thinking that Mom would be proud of us, getting things done without her.

Then that icy feeling hit, that this was the way it'd be going forward - without her. Make her proud. That mantra came into my brain and it's been there for all these decades. I'm sure it was there before, but now, it was a reason to go on. To stop those thoughts that "I can't, we can't make it without her."

If we did go on, and made her proud of us, from up in heaven, then that was a new purpose. As we drove to the funeral I thought it again – she'd be proud of how clean and dressed up everyone was for her Mass. She always liked that. She'd say, "We may not be the best dressed, but we can be clean and pressed."

We went back to the funeral home and waited there for the procession to the church. Her casket was open and we were all instructed to take one last look and say goodbye. Like she was really in there to say goodbye to us. Goodbye isn't one way. It takes two to say goodbye. Like that would somehow bring closure and we could "move on" – words I'd hear so many times in the upcoming months.

There was a lot of discussion over who would ride with whom in the fancy cars that the funeral home had there for us. There were so many of us, we couldn't all fit in one vehicle. I think Dad, Gary, Ann and Betty went in one and the three boys, Grandma and I went in the next. Then all the other close relatives drove themselves to the church, which in St. Libory was only two blocks from the funeral home, right down the street. We could have walked faster than this rigmarole took. This was the ceremony of burial and we were honoring the traditions - numbly, but we were trying.

The pall bearers were ready. I can't remember who they were. They had the awful job of lifting her casket into the hearse and into the church and to the cemetery, which in St. Libory is right next to the church. Convenient. I know they felt it an honor to carry her, and that's the right way to feel, I guess. I didn't want to touch the casket again.

The church bell tolled over and over as we marched into church. Dad first, followed by the seven of us. We sat in the first pew on the St. Joseph side of the church. Dad at the end, and we filled it up with our sadness. I had a pocket full of tissues and a handkerchief in my purse.

As we came into church I thought, "This is the fullest I've ever seen this place." All of the grade school kids were there, and lots of the residents of the town were kindly there for us. There were also people I didn't know that must have known Mom or Dad.

In the last pew stood Tom, my boyfriend and one of my new friends, Nancy. She had on this pretty white taffeta dress, and Tom was wearing a suit. I thought, "Wow, how nice of them to come." Nancy smiled at me through tears. I lost it when I saw them, crying hard all the way down the aisle to the front. I was touched to my soul that they came. To see them there made me feel like someone would still be there for me – when Mom no longer could be. That there would be others that would love and care about me, just me. Not like family that had to love you, but just me. That maybe my future would not just be this nightmarish numbness. All those thoughts came flooding in when I saw them at the back of the church. I sobbed all the way down the aisle.

Those hot tears just didn't stop. Try as I may, I couldn't get the sobbing that followed under control. Truth be told, I didn't really try. I felt like a tiny grain of sand in the universe as Mass started, like I might be swallowed up in some vortex and just disappear. The familiar words of the Catholic Mass sounded foreign. Why were we here again??

Oh no, it was still true. She was gone, and soon, she'd be in that cold, hard ground. I couldn't bear that thought. Never seeing her again. Never touching her skin or smelling her bread. Or hearing her laugh. It was not bearable. Let me die too. Take me, not her, to heaven with you, Lord, because she was needed here. The boys couldn't grow up without her. Dad didn't know us like she did, or know how to raise them.

Then, the anger came again, anger at both Him and Dad. I tried hard to put that down in my gut, because I was in His house and knew you could go to hell for being that disrespectful. I was sitting between Tommy and Danny. Both were just staring up at me, crying. I got myself together and blew my nose hard and wiped my eyes. I put my arms around them both. "Shame on you, Ellen, for indulging that crying fit – you need to be strong and get these little ones through this day," said the voice in my head. Mom. It was the first of many times I'd feel her presence, when I needed a good kick in the pants, when I needed a good hug or when I needed saving.

I looked over to the end of the pew. Dad was staring dead ahead, crying softly, tears dripping down his face and a little trickle of tears dripping from his nose. He was frozen. Not even blinking, not knowing. Just frozen. I handed a tissue to Gary and gestured to Dad's nose. Gary gave it to him and Dad didn't move. The tissue just laid on his hand. I thought maybe he couldn't move – like rigor mortis or a stroke. Then, he moved and wiped his eyes and nose.

I'd only seen my Dad cry once before Mom's death. Our farm dog, Poncho, was one of those great dogs that was both protective and gentle at once. He'd been with us as long as I could remember. When I was about 10 he had been caught in an animal trap, and his leg was mangled. When Dad found him, the dog was alive but just barely, and Dad had to shoot him to put him out of that pain.

Then Dad, always honest, had to tell his seven little ones that he'd shot their dog. He cried like a baby, and I remember thinking how soft his heart was inside. I never knew my strong, disciplinarian father cared so much about a dog. One of Dad's many sayings was, "Every good man gets one good dog and one good woman in this life, and I've had both."

The parish priest at St. Libory said the funeral Mass. All the Catholic traditions were performed. Lots of incense around the casket. Holy water sprinkled. As the water splattered on the casket, it felt like my heart was shattering into little pieces too.

The funeral prayers were said from the book. It was a High Mass, all sung, and the St. Libory choir was there to lead the singing, another surprise. They usually only sang for Sunday Mass, but Mom loved to sing and she liked that, I'm sure.

The priest gave a rambling sermon that didn't mention Mom's name. How awful that felt – she lived a short 40 years and had left seven children behind to show for it, and he didn't say her name or ours in his sermon. No nice words were said about what a good mother, wife, cook, seamstress, gardener, and sister, and all the other wonderful attributes she had were said. Nothing. Just his normal bullshit about sin and hell. Mom didn't have lots of sins (or at least not that this 14-year-old daughter knew about), so why preach about that on this day, her last day in this church?

I think disrespectful best describes how he delivered his sermon, and I was hurt. I vowed I'd never take another sacrament from him. This wasn't a mature view, but I wasn't mature; I was 14. I didn't marry in that beautiful church, my home church, for that reason, choosing Okawville's church and priest instead six years later when I got married.

Mass was finally over, and the pallbearers lifted her up. The priest led the procession to the cemetery, followed by the pallbearers and then Dad and the seven of us. We were followed by most of those in church. The school kids were dismissed back to their classes. It was nice they were there for the service. Mom would have liked them there, singing loudly for her. The walk to the cemetery was short, but seemed to take forever, following her casket.

The boys were crying hard now, and I didn't try to stop them. I was crying too. I think the whole assemblage may have been. All I could think about was the ground and the bugs that maybe would get inside her coffin. The cold that was coming, surrounding her, and the baby that lay with her; he'd be so cold too. How could this be fair, how could this be happening? This was not supposed to be the way this turned out. Make this dream end. STOP IT!!

Then we were at the gravesite. Green carpet, or something like a rug, had been placed, and there were chairs we were instructed to sit on in a row in front of the casket. There was a big hole in the ground – with the dirt to one side that they'd removed to dig the hole. Oh, this was scary – this was the end. She'd go in and I'd really never see her again. NO! Please stop this dream now. Just let me run down that hill and into that stream and let me float away from this. No, get a grip on yourself, Ellen, take Danny's hand; he doesn't know where to sit. Get him to sit down and you sit down too. You can't go anywhere. It's almost over.

More incense. It was nauseating and I hadn't eaten breakfast, so I was feeling sick. More Catholic prayers. All these prayers, and still she's dead.

Finally, the last song was finished and they motioned for Dad to stand up. He took a handful of dirt and placed it on the coffin. We all followed him and placed a little dirt on her. The symbolism of, "Remember, man, that you are dust and unto dust you shall return," was important to our faith.

I was so glad they didn't lower her all the way in, just kind of rested her on the top of the ground. I knew they'd do it after we left. I just was glad not to see her go all the way in. Into that cold dirt.

It was finished.

Chapter 5

We Go On

The ladies of the St. Libory Rosary Sodality put out a great funeral lunch in the church basement. I remember Mom's pride when she'd bring her cakes to the lunches for others. I wonder what she thought of the spread that day. The family and close friends stayed, and the ladies were so kind. This tradition was an important part of "moving on" – getting back to normal after a death. It was just nice, too, not to go straight home to more tears. It was much better to have lots of people around to try to drown out the memory of the last two hours of hell at the funeral Mass.

There were cakes of all kinds and summer sausage and, of course, "funeral dogs." These were special hot dogs made by the local meat market, Wennemans. They were longer than normal hot dogs, with a natural casing we called "skin" on them, and they were delicious. They still are! I love them, but that day I couldn't eat one. I chose a piece of cake and some Jell-O. The boys all chomped down on the funeral dogs. I thought, "Some things won't change, like the three boys' appetites." They were little eating machines then already, only to get more so as they grew.

It almost felt normal, all the relatives around us, and the school basement I'd grown up in. It felt good to have that place around me. Nancy and Tom didn't stay, as they had to get back to classes. Nancy hugged me so hard when she left I thought I'd pass out. In the months ahead, I'd lean on her and talk with her about how I felt with Mom gone, like I did with no one else. I'd stay at her house overnight often and her parents were always kind, patient and loving. She was the youngest and only child at home. Their home was calm and quiet. It was so different than the normal chaos present in a home of nine, no now eight, people that was my "normal." I always felt welcome and cared for at Nancy's house.

We went home after the lunch. Dad looked just wiped out – I'd never seen him that way before. He went right to bed, telling the extended family that had come home with us, "You can stay if you want. I'm going to sleep now."

Dad let us stay out of school the rest of the week. Maybe he wanted us to have some time, maybe it was comforting to have us all near. He seemed lost, like he was seeing things in our house for the first time. For some things, maybe he was. Things started changing.

Take the laundry, for example. He realized pretty quickly that not having a dryer was a huge issue. This made me mad, sad and glad all at once. Mom had begged him for an electric dryer for years, and now he just went out and bought one. I'm not sure where Dad got the money for this and for the other changes. I was grateful not to have to hang clothes all over the basement, which in the winter really didn't work well, but so sad that now we had it after she was gone. Every time I loaded it, it hurt.

The aunts came that week. It seemed like they'd set up a schedule, because someone was there each day. I thought, "They have families, how can they do this?" Then, realized pretty quickly it was just for this week, to help us get through the first hard patch of Mom not being there. Aunt Veronica, one of Dad's sisters, was there ironing one day. She must think I am really lazy, I thought, as I read in the back bedroom. But, I just couldn't make myself help her iron. I felt heavy, like I weighed a ton and moving was hard.

I was into James Taylor. I liked the softness of his voice and his lyrics. His song "Fire and Rain" was on the top hit list the fall of 1970. To this day I tear up when I hear it – "I always thought I'd see you, one more time again...." I had the "45" and we had a small, portable record player that scratched like crazy, but it worked. Mom got that James Taylor record and a Johnny Cash one for me for my birthday in July. I played the song over and over and cried and cried until I thought I had no tears left for the rest of my life, but they came again the next time I played it.

While Aunt Maryann was there, I remember watching TV with the three boys, and there was something funny on – and we all laughed out loud. "Oh, no, we can't do that," I thought, realizing it was the first time since she'd died that the house had that sound. Laughing was just wrong now, something I thought I'd never feel like doing again. I'm grateful time heals that feeling, but at the time I didn't know it would.

Dad must have gone to the school sometime before we went back to classes, because I remember helping the boys with their homework, so they wouldn't be behind when they went back. It would be just one week after we buried her.

The school bus had never come all the way down to our house. It stopped at our neighbor's house. We walked the mile or so to their house to catch the bus, or Mom drove us. Dad had a running fight with the school district to have the bus come to our house. I don't remember the reason they refused, only that it made Dad so mad, at "them," which I took to be the "establishment" (remember this is the '70s). It was a public road with our mail box at the end, so there was no real argument they could sustain to refuse to come to the end of it, but Dad lost his battle with them every year. Only after Mom died, they changed their mind without him even asking again, and the bus came right to our door.

I remember Dad wasn't happy to have "won" and was upset at how it got accomplished. The look on his face reflected a feeling of defeat. However, he didn't protest, and the big yellow bus pulled right up to the circle drive that Dad had made for it at the end of our driveway.

Another change happened in the kitchen. Cooking had always been Mom's department, other than barbequing and occasional breakfasts. Those were the only things Dad knew how to cook, or to my knowledge had ever cooked. I don't think he had ever gone grocery shopping either. The three girls had helped Mom cook for years, so we knew our way around most of the kitchen. We knew we had lots of meat and produce in the freezer to get us through the first winter, and Mom had been canning all summer before she died. There just wasn't the time after school to bake the ham or the roast beef she'd have been working on during the day. So, we resorted to lots of hamburgers, baked in the oven on a cookie sheet, for dinner. Mom's wonderful pot of oatmeal with bacon or her pancakes and sausages became cold cereal and milk for breakfast most days.

Thank God that Aunt Loretta was a cook at a nearby parochial school, as she brought us leftovers often. We so enjoyed the pizza, spaghetti and other goodies she'd bring us as she checked in on us each evening on her way home from work. She was always there for us with food and her time. She wasn't like Mom, a nurturer with a hug, but we knew she cared and were grateful for her help during the years after we lost Mom.

Lunches we'd always taken from home – summer sausage on homemade bread, with a cookie or two, if we were good. School lunches were an extravagance for richer folks than us. The necessity of getting us all out of the house without Mom there directing changed that – and we ate school lunches now most of the time. I know we would have qualified for the free lunch program, but that was not ever discussed, no handouts for us Muellers. And, I'm grateful

Dad stuck to that lesson for us. We didn't have a Mom anymore, but we at least had that little bit of dignity.

Dad was employed by Kozarek Construction in New Athens as a pile driver and worked whenever there was a job available for him. Carpentry work, even in the union, is always seasonal. I'm not sure how he found the money for the cases of Cap'n Crunch cereal and the school lunches, but he did. I'm surprised we all grew and were healthy, as our diet quickly became carb-laden, with few fruits or vegetables. Diabetes was in our family history, and only Gary, the oldest, developed it later in life, so we have been blessed.

I don't think Dad had any idea of the work my Mom did until she wasn't there. The daily cooking, laundry, cleaning, homework - all of it was so much for one person. And especially one person that hadn't been involved in any of this. It had to be truly difficult for Dad. I can't imagine how overwhelmed he felt. My sisters and I did help to keep the three little boys going, with baths, cooking, homework, but Dad did a lot too.

I could have helped more, but I was still so mad at him that I chose not to. Mom wouldn't have died if he hadn't gotten her pregnant, so this was all his fault.

Chapter 6

Back to "Normal"

I dreaded going back to high school. Okawville Community High School was not a big place – there were just 60 or so students in my class. Everyone knew everyone. I dreaded those looks of pity. Our family went to church together on Sunday and everyone stared as we came in – and I felt like melting. They were not mean stares, just "those poor children" stares. No one talked to us after Mass, just gave us those stares, like they didn't know what to say.

High school was much of the same. Some people just avoided me, it seemed, and wouldn't make eye contact. Maybe they didn't know what to say, either. That hurt. Several people came up to me and offered their sympathy, or asked if I was okay. I remember standing at my locker just frozen after the third person came up, Danny. He was a really cute and nice boy in my Freshman class, and I didn't know him very well. He asked, "How are you, are you and your family doing okay?" I mumbled, "Yes, we are doing okay." My head was pounding; I just wanted things back to normal, to this not happening.

I just wanted Mom to be back to talk with that night, to tell her all about the new friends I'd made, and to not have this numbness anymore. The bell rang and I could not move. Nancy was down a few lockers, and when she came over, I just could not keep back the tears. Home Economics was our next class, and she was in it with me. The teacher kindly let her take me into the kitchen. I felt so embarrassed. Attention was not what I wanted, just for it to not have happened, to go away! That wasn't going to happen, so I managed to compose myself and join the class.

Years later I learned that Danny had lost his mother at an even younger age than I did. He was just being kind. His twin sister, Debbie and I later became close friends for life. Sharing the loss of your mom creates a strong bond.

The rest of the week was a blur. I don't remember even being at school. The following week seemed to get back to feeling a little more "normal," if one could call this dull ache in my heart and my hiding of it from everyone "normal". A routine returned, with helping at home and my schoolwork and activities.

Dad was more distant than ever, seeming to not talk at all when he got home from work exhausted. He had never been a hugger, demonstrative in any way, or verbal about his love for his children. But we knew he did. Now, he seemed not to know what to say to any of us, so nothing was said. I sensed he was trying so hard to set the brave example, knowing he had to keep it together or we'd all fall apart.

The aunts, other than Loretta, went back to their own families and lives, as they needed to. We were a sad little flock of eight, on our own.

Mid-term grades came out in the middle of October and I was shocked with my Chemistry grade. It was a "D." There had only been two grades taken, and I'd gotten A's, so I was not expecting this at all. The science instructor for our Freshman Chemistry class was a wonderful teacher, firm and fair. His classes were hard but we learned in them and I enjoyed the class. I went to talk with him, thinking there'd been a mistake.

He said, no, I'd missed the main test for the quarter. I asked when it was, and he said it had been on September 30. I had no idea there was a test, much less that I had missed it. I stood dumbstruck looking at him and said, "My Mom died, I was out of school." I thought maybe he didn't know. He calmly said he did know, but I hadn't asked to make it up, and it wasn't his job to tell me. He said he'd let me make up the test, which was against his policy, but given the circumstances he'd allow it.

While I was grateful for the makeup test, I was taken aback at how matter-of-factly he spoke. It was the first time I'd heard someone else, someone I didn't know well, talk about Mom being dead, and it brought that nightmarish feeling back so quickly I gasped. I tried so hard not to cry, but I was so hurt by his manner. It was like he was telling me it was sunny outside or some simple fact, not that he knew my mother was dead. I couldn't stop those hot tears that rolled down my face. He looked down, pretending not to notice my tears. I was so mad at myself for crying. I said, "Thank you," and he said to come back the next hour after class.

I didn't have time to study, but took the test and got a high C on it. I'm not super smart, but I really studied hard to make A's. My grade was a B for the first quarter, the only B I'd ever gotten on a report card. That B ended up bringing down my rank in our graduating class of 1974 to number three, instead of my being tied with the valedictorian and salutatorian.

The Homecoming Dance was on December 5, 1970, my first-ever high school dance. Ann had gone the year before. She had had a date, and Mom had made her a cute new dress. Our neighbor, who was a hairdresser, had even come over and put her hair in a grownup up-do. I was so excited to have my turn for my first dance and have Mom spoil me, too. I'm sure she would have if she'd been there.

As it turned out, I borrowed a dress from the sister of another new friend, Peggy. It was a long blue dress that was two sizes too big for me. I was voted the Freshman Attendant, and Tom, my boyfriend, was my escort. I was honored to be part of the dance's court, but still wonder if it was a "pity" vote. Anyway, I think Mom would have been thrilled to see me at the ceremony before the dance. We had to make three big bows, all the way to the floor, to those attending in the bleachers and to the retiring queen. I was so scared I'd mess it up, as I was pretty clumsy (and still am). I practiced over and over, and it went okay that night.

I asked Dad if he'd come for the ceremony. He looked at me like "What for?" and he didn't show up. I don't think he had any idea it was important for a parent to be there. All the other kids in the court had their parents beaming there.

I missed Mom that night and realized this was the first of many big events in my life she'd miss. If we'd not lost her, she'd have made sure both she and Dad had come.

Mother's Days have always been the hardest. Even once we had our two precious children and everything in the world to be grateful for, I'd long for her on that day. Even once my mother-in-law Doris (I married that cute boy from High School World History class, Bill Krohne, in 1976) became my Mom in every way, I still felt this hole in my heart. Especially on Mother's Day. I always will.

Home was unbearable during that winter of 1970. There was a sadness that permeated every inch of our little farm house. Winter is usually overcast and grey in Illinois, and this winter seemed especially dark. Dad was laid off, like every winter. He was so distant. He was drinking a lot. It was his way of coping, I guess.

One way I coped was to be super busy. It kept the pain away. I joined every club and extra-curricular activity I could at school. I spent time at Nancy's. I got a job at the OK Drive-Inn, a hamburger and ice-cream restaurant in Okawville. I took every class I could, just wanting to be busy. When I was busy working or at an activity, I couldn't think of Mom and the pain. This "busy equals happy" mindset has stuck with me. It's hard for me to do nothing and just relax. My family teases that I have CSS: "Can't Sit Still."

By the end of my junior year in high school, I had enough credits to graduate. My friend Sue did as well, so we petitioned the school board to allow us to graduate in the middle of our senior year. Dad had to go with me to the meeting with the school board as no one had ever done this before. I remember being grateful for his support, even if it was just to get me out of the house as soon as he could. Dad was clear we, especially the girls, should leave home by age 18. Sue was all set to go to nursing school. Heading to Belleville Area College with no clue of a major or what I wanted to do became my next step.

But there were a few tough years to get through first.

Chapter 7

It Gets Worse

Late in the fall after Mom's death, I overheard Dad talking with Grandma Mueller about "splitting us up." Someone had suggested, I'm not sure who, to have different sisters of his take the three little boys to raise in their families. Maybe go to each of their godparents. No one wanted the older kids. Sure, we were teenagers, but we had been pretty good until then. Teenagers, especially girls, need a mom. It hurt. They rationalized, we older ones shouldn't change high schools, and we could stay with Dad.

I couldn't even bear to think about being separated from the three little boys. They were doing okay, their report cards were good, and Mom would have been proud. We older ones had all worked hard to be sure they were fed, bathed, dressed and their homework was done. I was so hurt. All of this wasn't good enough – they were going to take them away. It just couldn't happen! I talked with Gary and Ann – we had to stop this. They'd already lost their mom, now to lose their brothers and sisters and the farm they knew as home (even as sad as it was right now) was just not right, in my mind.

The three of us confronted Dad. I was ready for a fight, but didn't get one. He agreed. He didn't want to lose us either or have the boys go anywhere else. The seven of us would be better together than separated. We'd get through this together, somehow. He looked so overwhelmed, so sad, so hollow-eyed, not like Dad at all. I can't imagine how he felt, scared at this single parent responsibility for which he wasn't prepared. Mourning his wife, his love, and a son he'd never know. Regretting some things, maybe. I'll never know, because he didn't talk about his feelings then or ever with me. He didn't split us up and for that I'll always respect and be grateful to him.

Dad did have a breakdown, though. It was just too much - for anyone. He passed out one night at home. The ambulance came and in muffled tones a "nervous breakdown" was mentioned. I remember him being gone, in the hospital for several days. Just when it seemed things couldn't possibly get worse, now Dad wasn't here either.

Before he came home from the hospital, a woman came to our house. Grandma, Aunt Loretta, Gary, Ann and I were to meet with this woman. She was from social services – worried about seven kids alone on a farm with a father in an unstable mental state. Aunt Loretta and we three girls cleaned the house top to bottom, and the boys were in their best school clothes for the visit. The lady seemed nice enough, but Aunt Loretta had instructed us to not trust her - to tell her everything was okay and we were just fine, which, I think in physical ways, we were. None of us was dealing with the grief we hid well, but we were getting on with life and doing okay at holding in the pain.

The woman asked lots of questions about our daily routines and who did what around the house. We must have passed the test, because she left and we didn't hear from her or anyone else again. Dad came home, but he didn't work for a few more days. He seemed somehow better than before. I don't know if they gave him medication, talked with him about his grief, or what happened during his days away. I just know it seemed better, like he had somehow turned a page.

It sank in after that episode that we'd better stick together, or we'd be taken apart.

Christmas was approaching. Mom never made a big deal about some holidays, like Halloween – some costumes were recycled, and we usually just went trick-or-treating at Grandma's and at the neighbors' houses down our road. We managed that just fine with the boys. Thanksgiving was always at Grandma Mueller's house, and that wasn't changed. Christmas, that was different.

Christmas was the holiday our Mom and whole family loved. Christ's birth. And Santa Claus. And the smells – Mom baked sugar cookies, maraschino cherry cookies and special breads just for Christmas. The smells would fill the house for the week before. She'd wrap packages of decorated sugar cookies for our teachers and write a note of gratitude to each one. We would deliver them to our teachers on the last day of class before the holiday.

There were lots of church activities, from the school Christmas pageant to choir practice. And on Christmas Day, we visited both sides of the family. But my favorite part of Christmas was Christmas Eve.

On Christmas Eve morning, Dad would take the boys and chop down an evergreen tree in the pasture, and then Mom and the girls would decorate it. We had one string of big colored bulbs, a couple dozen glass ornaments, lots of homemade ornaments from school projects and tinsel. Lots of tinsel. I thought our tree was the prettiest one every year.

Then, after an early supper, Dad would hang a quilt from the doorframe between the living room and the kitchen. We'd go off to church. When we got back from church, a miracle had occurred and Santa Claus had come to our house. There was always a little pile of presents for each of us kids. They were not wrapped, just in a neat little pile. In order around the tree from oldest to youngest child. We'd run to ours, quickly figuring out which were our treasures. New colors, a coloring book, maybe a book all our own, socks, and one special toy. One year I got a Barbie doll and Betty got a Penny Brite doll. The boys got a tractor or blocks. The year before Mom died, the boys all got "tommy guns." They loved them.

In 1970, there was no tree. No tinsel. We should have insisted for the boys' sake. Dad just couldn't do it. We baked a batch of sugar cookies, so we did keep one tradition alive. We had set up the nativity scene that Mom loved, with the little painted donkeys and cows and the baby Jesus.

We went to church together after supper, and when we came home, Dad called us all together in the living room. Dad pulled a large bag out from his bedroom. I was shocked and touched that he'd bought us gifts. For the three girls, he had bathrobes. One was pink with big roses, one was plain pink, and one was green with yellow braiding down the front. They were all about the same size, too big for us, but that didn't matter. Dad had bought us them, and they were precious. Dad hadn't put our names on them, and when he said we could each pick the one we wanted, I grabbed the green and yellow one.

As soon as I did, I regretted it – I should have let Betty or Ann pick first. But, it was so pretty, and I just wanted it. They both wanted that one too, I could tell, but they didn't make a fuss about it. I confessed my selfishness to the priest the next week and he gave me a harsh penance – many prayers. It was not enough; I still feel badly all these years later.

My anger at Dad softened as he worked his way through getting healthier after the nervous breakdown. It was surreal that we never talked about it – as though it just hadn't happened. I figured that was just the way men were. None that I knew expressed their emotions.

My anger at Mom's death took a new bent, one I wasn't expecting to be so vehement.

I was angry at God. I was not at all sure how He, who is so all-powerful, could find any reason in the world to take our mom. At 14, I couldn't comprehend the Why of this, and it tore me apart inside. Church had always been a constant in our lives. We never missed Sunday Mass and our grade school classes went to church daily. I turned to the church for answers. I'm not sure what I expected to find. I sure wasn't going to go and talk to the parish priest.

So, I just went to church and prayed. I asked Jesus to give me the answer to Why Mom died and how we'd go on. I went with Aunt Loretta every Wednesday evening during that Lenten season and went to every service during Holy Week. Surely by Easter I'd have a revelation. I prayed so hard and sometimes couldn't help crying a little. I sat by myself in our pew on the right-hand side of the church, where Mom and Dad always sat with all of us. The plaster walls were as cold as my heart.

I prayed He'd answer me, help me make sense of this. Easter came and went – but no answer. I became even madder at Him, now really not sure what to do or who else to ask for an answer.

I gave up – just quit my prayers. I started thinking He wasn't real or at least wasn't the kind, loving God that I was taught about for all those years. It was all a lie, a big fat lie. I didn't like this conclusion to my vigil for understanding. It wasn't comfortable, and I hated even thinking these thoughts - only to myself, of course, not out loud or to share with others. I harbored this extra hate for a while and was worried that it was settling across my normally happy outlook on life.

I had never questioned my faith before. For most of my life, everyone I knew was Catholic, but now I'd met friends in high school that weren't. Nancy was something called a United Church of Christ member; others were Lutheran or Baptist. Dad said all these were not good, not real religions and to stay away from them and never even think of marrying someone who wasn't Catholic.

But I was questioning now. Big time. And I was scared of the answers. I couldn't put it all together in my brain – the loving God we trust and this horrible act of taking her from us. Why? People said things like, "She's in a better place," "She's with him in heaven," "It was her time to go home." All that was just crap. Her place was with us, to raise her seven kids, not to leave us alone with Dad. How were we ever going to get to college and be normal kids? Dad loved us, but we needed Mom. God had lots of other angels – He didn't need her. Others suggested, "He doesn't give you more than you can handle – what doesn't kill you makes you stronger." At 14, I didn't buy any of that.

I'm not sure what I'd have done with this anger and doubt, if it weren't for Nancy. She invited me to the United Church of Christ DuBois Center for a teen retreat weekend when I was a junior in high school. I didn't tell Dad I was going – just that I was at Nancy's for the weekend. He would not have let me go – it wasn't Catholic. But, I think most of the time he was just glad to have me out of the house, instead of there talking back to him.

The retreat was fun. The DuBois Center was, and still is, a beautiful, tree-filled property that even had a lake with a rope bridge. A peaceful place. The leaders of the retreat didn't push religion. They just talked about a couple of Bible verses and we were asked to reflect on them. I remember one from the Gospel of John about how "God is love." They explained that He shows His love for us in all different ways. Sometimes ways we can't understand or even try to. Always with love in His heart. Always with us in His heart.

This was so different than our Catholic services. I opened myself up and cried all night. I felt new, like I did at my confirmation. I had met some new friends there and felt safe to talk with them about my hateful heart. It helped to take it away. I let out that horrible pain I was holding, the hate that had been building in me. I felt hopeful again, hopeful the pain could stop. The next day we had more discussions, and I felt that love coming back into my heart for Him. For everyone.

It's what I would call an "AHA!" a "light bulb moment" years later in my consulting career. I just knew it felt good to have Jesus back in my heart.

The only issue with the weekend was that I got a very bad case of bronchitis so I missed a whole week of school. Maybe that happened to let those lessons sink in while I recuperated. I remember that Dad brought me soup and asked if I was okay in a kind way. It was not how he usually acted when you were sick. His philosophy was, "get up and get to work, you'll get better." Whatever the reason for my illness, I felt better in my heart than I had since Mom passed. I felt like I could at least go on and hope for a happy life. I still missed her so much, but the anger was gone.

Chapter 8

Saving

I knew Mom was in heaven, or at least I felt evidence of that from some very scary incidents in my life. Maybe this evidence of my belief is more spiritual than physical. I hesitated to include this chapter, because I'm afraid you, dear reader, will think less of my sanity. You'll have to trust me that I am sane and well-grounded. I've included these stories - and there are some experiences in my sibling's chapters, too, - in the hope that they will confirm for any of you that have also felt your loved one's presence, that you are not alone in this special experience.

I'd felt her presence at the school gym the night she died. Or at least I felt strongly that something had happened: I was not sure what. I heard her at the funeral, telling me to help my little brothers. All through the years I'd written to her in my journal and talked to her in my head, asking her what she thought of issues, of people. Asking for guidance on what she'd want me to do. Sometimes, once I'd talked through things with her, I'd feel a calmness that I came to attribute to her "being there with me." Guiding me. I worried sometimes that this wasn't "normal," but it made me able to function without her, so I didn't care if it wasn't.

I wore yellow, the color she chose for my clothes as she sewed them, because it made me feel close to her. Who knew this would turn into a lifelong yellow obsession!

There were three very clear times I felt the presence and protection of God through "feeling my mother's help."

By the time I turned 16, I'd saved enough money to buy a car. That was Dad's requirement, one that I thought was so appropriate, Bill and I did it with our own children. We had to earn enough money to buy a car before we could get a driver's license. I had saved $300 from working at the OK Drive-Inn. Dad took it and brought home a blue 1957 Chevy Impala, a big "boat" of a car. It was all mine and represented real freedom. I could go when I wanted and not have to beg rides from friends or my brother Gary or Aunt Loretta all the time.

Betty and I were both working at the OK Drive-Inn. We left home for work on a hot summer Saturday morning just as it was starting to rain. By the time we got to the Venedy blacktop road, on our way to Okawville, it was pouring. We were running late, so I was speeding, going about 65 miles per hour. I lost control on the hot, wet blacktop that now had a thin coat of oil covering it – and my car swerved back and forth and finally flipped over several times in the deep roadside ditch. We were hydroplaning. I was told later how dangerous those driving conditions were. I just didn't know.

Betty and I both remember the crash and flipping over. We woke up, upside down in the big ditch beside the road. I remember a very calm, peaceful feeling, not scared at all. I "felt" Mom there, lifting us up, and when we stopped, Betty and I were both in the back seat. The vacuum cleaner that we had in the back seat was completely crushed in what was left of the front passenger seat. The front of the car was completely demolished. There was no way we could have gotten to the back seat like that ourselves, no way we should have survived that crash.

Just by coincidence (or maybe divine intervention, too) my friend Nancy came upon the accident first. She was who we saw when we crawled out of the back seat and she hugged us both as we shook and cried in the pouring rain. I don't remember how, but she got her Dad there quickly and he took us in to town, to the OK Drive-Inn. We didn't even have a scratch.

I was scared to death to call Dad, but did when we got to work and he called a tow truck to get the car. I didn't know how badly the car had been damaged, until someone came into the OK Drive-Inn and asked who'd been killed in that blue Chevy that was now at the local body shop down the street.

Our boss, Elaine, said we should go home and rest. We were not hurt at all, just shaken up, and I didn't want to see Dad. I was sure he would be furious. We worked our shift, and Dad came and picked us up that afternoon. He wasn't mad at all – he just said that he was grateful we were okay, and explained how to drive in the rain. I was grateful Mom had saved us, but didn't tell Dad, or anyone, about the feeling I had had. But it was very real to me. When I asked Betty about it recently, she remembered being in the back seat when we stopped, but not feeling Mom's presence.

The next time I had the experience of her presence was again in an accident. I was 18. I'd been dating a slightly older guy from Clinton County. His friends had motorcycles, and one evening one of his friends asked if I'd like a ride. I said sure. No helmet or protective gear, we were just out for a little ride down some backroads. Suddenly, there was a car ahead coming towards us. I guess the driver didn't see us because they ran us off the small backroad, right into a corn field. We both flew off of the bike into the muddy field that had just been harvested. I landed face down in the stubble.

When I came to, I looked up, and my head was less than an inch from a large wooden electric pole, about 18 inches in diameter. Again, I felt this very calm presence and knew the protection of God through Mom had prevented me from hitting it. I was filthy from the freshly harvested field, but had no broken bones, no cuts, nothing. Another inch and I'd have been dead for sure. I lay there breathing, thanking God and her for being there.

The driver couldn't understand why I was so happy when he regained consciousness and found me. I never rode a motorcycle again, and I don't intend to. After that incident, I felt like I should find purpose in my life. She must be saving me for some reason, right?

The third time I felt her presence was at the birth of our son, Ab. I was 30. It had been a very hard labor. The labor had been induced, so it came on very quickly. This was in the days before spinals or drugs were routinely used and "natural childbirth" was the norm. Bill had been so excited by our first child, Joy's, birth five years earlier, he hardly realized how much pain I was in. But his face showed he knew now. One final push and, "It's a boy!" were joyous words.

Then nothing. No baby cries. The nurses and doctor looked solemn. I screamed in panic, "What's wrong?"

Then I heard the doctor say, "Cord's wrapped. Get oxygen."

I saw the baby – all blue, like death. I laid back and begged God to let him be okay. I prayed, "God, please, Mom, please, we need you now. He can't be like Robert and not make it." Suddenly, a calmness came over me, I knew it would be okay. I felt that presence and protection.

Then we heard this tiny whimper, barely a cry, but knew he was okay.

I never told Bill or anyone that I'd felt that presence at Ab's birth. Or that I spoke to her regularly. It was as though telling anyone was a violation of an unspoken covenant.

My rational brain knows that it is in my believing that she is there, that the presence and protection of God is. That's enough for me. My belief is strong that she's been there for me, in these times and throughout my life as I've asked her for guidance. That confirms my faith in God. I think He really doesn't take people from us. Perhaps He just lets us know them and lets them help us in different ways.

Chapter 9

Healing

The next time I'd consciously work on healing from Mom's death was many years later.

I was in my 40s and living in Hillsboro, Illinois with my husband, Bill, and our two beautiful children, Joy and Ab. I'd been so fortunate in life and felt truly blessed. Bill was a loving husband, my partner in life. I had a great job at Illinois Power and was advancing in my management career.

After Joy was born, I had another "AHA!" moment. While telling my first newborn baby all the things she could become, I realized I wasn't a good example. I didn't even have my college degree. I'd dropped out after a year, when my savings ran out, and went to work full time. So, Bill and I made the decision that I would go back to school. I started with one or two nights a week at Belleville Area College and then continued with National Lewis University. Working full time and raising a family, we were busy! It took me nine years but getting my bachelor's degree was worth it. I was certain Mom would have been proud of that accomplishment. I was working hard on my master's degree online at the University of Phoenix.

I was also blessed in the "Mom" department. Bill's mother, Doris, was like a Mom to me from the time we met. She helped me plan our wedding and bought me the perfect dress. She babysat our children. Neither she nor Bill's

Dad, Ab, judged or offered advice unless asked. She was a great mother-in-law and friend and I loved them both dearly.

My siblings were all doing well too. The "three little boys" had graduated from college and were all married, had children, and were doing well. Annie had married and settled down following her tumultuous years after Mom's death, and she had two boys and a fine husband too. Betty had twins and was my best friend. She was working on her bachelor's degree and lived near us. Gary ran a small business and had "overachieved" the most, with four children.

We stayed close, getting together for all of the major holidays and often in between. We watched each other's children, visited, and carried on the tradition of raucous laughter when we were together. The stories of our childhood were relayed to the next generation, including Dad's theory on genetics and various silliness from our growing up. We'd survived the worst and were close, all scarred in our own ways from the trauma of Mom's death and the grief we would carry for life. But we were together.

Bill and I had moved away from our hometown of Okawville to follow my career with Illinois Power, but we were always within driving distance of family. Only my brother Tom moved out of the region to Knoxville, Tennessee, where he is a professor at the University of Tennessee. He and his family came back to the area for the important family events and gatherings.

My brother Bill was an attorney and had started his own firm in Belleville, Illinois with his wife, Kathy. They were very involved in these Catholic retreats called Koinonia, which is a Greek word for community. I agreed to go to the Koinonia to satisfy my brother Bill's frequent asking.

A Koinonia is a retreat led by lay Catholics that have attended in the past. It consists of services in the chapel, prayer time, speakers that talk openly about their struggles with life and with God, time for reflection on one's beliefs and lots of food during a long weekend. They were held in Springfield, Illinois, on beautiful wooded grounds surrounded by a lake. The building was stately with wide windows framing expansive views. It is just a peace-filled setting.

Bill had asked me many times to go to one of these retreats, and I was just too busy. I didn't really need a retreat to work on anything, right? Well, as the retreat unfolded, it opened all of those old feelings of sadness and the insatiable Why from which I'd not fully healed. As the lights were dimmed in the chapel and we prayed aloud together, I opened my heart. I began to realize that these wounds never fully heal. They just scab over nicely and unless picked at, don't fester. A griever is a griever for life, just with different levels of intensity as we work on resolving our grief.

That retreat let me continue the work I'd started years ago at the teen retreat at the DuBois Center, thinking about God's love and renewing my faith in Him and the goodness of the world. Bill, Kathy and I had long talks, and Ann and Dan, who'd already attended a Koinonia, joined us that evening during the family ceremony. I wept like a baby when I saw them. The experience was cleansing away my pain, buried deeply, and pulling me closer to them and to Him. I felt happier than I had in a long, long time.

My sister Betty went with me to the next Koinonia. Betty and I went to several, and I helped lead some of the sessions, talking about Mom and the pain our family went through, just as my brother Bill had done at my first retreat. With the help of the Gospel of John's "God is Love" message, sharing our experience and my struggle was cathartic. I hoped I was helping others in their journey with the Lord and through any pain in the grief they had encountered.

I am grateful for my Mom and Dad's steadfast religious upbringing. Time and again in my life, as adversity was ahead for me, prayer helped to guide my direction. As you will read in my sibling's stories in the chapters ahead, their faith pulled many of them through too.

When Bill and I were married just over a year, I became pregnant. We had talked about having a family but were surprised I was pregnant so soon. I'd had ovarian cysts removed right after we were married, and the doctor said it may be hard for us to conceive. I'd had some heavy bleeding in the third month of my pregnancy, but the local doctor thought all was okay. At my fourth month visit, he didn't hear a heartbeat and the sonogram confirmed I'd miscarried.

I felt so guilty for the loss of the baby. I must have done something wrong to have lost the baby. I'd fallen off my bike in my eighth week, could that have done it? I kept going full speed ahead, like always, not resting like maybe I should have. Was that it? The doctors had no answers, just that these things happen. I was so sad, so down, unable to focus and not my happy self at all. While I was questioning God on Why, it was in a hopeful way, not hate-filled, as I had in Mom's death. I trusted it would work out all right.

After 18 months and I still wasn't pregnant, we were worried. I'd developed complications after the surgery the doctor performed after the miscarriage and another surgery followed. We were scared that Bill and I may not be blessed to be parents. My sister Betty became a mother while we waited and prayed. She was gentle in her joy with me, knowing I was hurting.

Bill was so kind and did special things to get me through the grief of the miscarriage. He knew my love of traveling, so we took a trip to Arkansas and another to Florida. He was hurting too, but we were together in the pain. Once we did finally become pregnant, he took good care of me when I became bed-ridden in the first trimester.

The grief from the miscarriage was hard, but I can't even comprehend the impact of losing a child you'd had the fortune to hold and love, and I pray never to find out.

When our parents passed, Bill and I held on to each other. I prayed when Bill's parents got ill, and as they suffered, I knew He was there for them. When my Dad passed after a long battle with leukemia, I didn't question, just prayed and grieved for him.

Reflecting on these experiences with grief later in my life, it's clear that the difference between hope and despair in grief is having someone like Bill by my side, loving me through it. Having good friends to listen to me cry and hug me, time and again, such as my friends Debbie and Jules did at my miscarriage, makes a huge difference. And as an adult, having matured in my thinking, I was now better equipped to grieve than I was as a teenager.

These experiences with grief reinforced for me how important it is to tell those we love, that we do. To not wait to tell them, as I did with my Mom. I learned from losing her that we can't just let the days pass and not appreciate those we love. Or, wait to do the things we think are important in or with our lives. Because each day may be our last day.

I also learned that I have control over my feelings and my words. I had the ability to choose not to hate, Dad or God, and to move on from those feelings with God's peace. I have the ability to be happy each day or not - my choice. To be a screamer and argue loudly or to work on peacefully compromising in my marriage. Most days I look for what's right and move forward joyfully. Not always, but I try harder than I think I would have if I'd had Mom with me into adulthood.

Mom sang often. She sang "Zip-A-Dee-Doo-Dah" to us as she took us to the bus stop each morning. A song of that hope for joy. "My, oh my, what a wonderful day, plenty of sunshine heading our way." I sang it to my children while taking them to school, and when things get hard, it's my go-to. Little things mean a lot when they are no more, like hearing her sing that song. I was able to honor her in 2000 at an assemblage for working women, The Women's Conference in Champaign, Illinois, where I sang that song in her memory to 2,000 women as I introduced a speaker as an Illinois Power executive. Believe me, it was scary because I didn't get any of the singing genes!

I also learned how important it is to have both parents involved in the parenting process. While Dad was a loving father, he was not involved in caring for us – that was Mom's job. After she died, he had a steep learning curve on how to parent his seven children.

When Bill and I got married, I knew I wanted to be a working person even when we had children, to be able to make money and not be reliant on his income. When we had Joy and later Ab, Bill was a very hands-on father from day one. He fed, diapered and bathed them right along with me. He was there with them when they were sick and cared for them while I was at night school getting my degree. They would all be fine if something were to happen to me. That was important. I feel blessed to have been there for all of those important and everyday events in my children's lives that my Mom missed with us, but I knew they'd be okay if I weren't, because Bill is an awesome dad.

In writing these words and remembering those feelings 47 years later, I feel blessed to have taken this opportunity to figure out how her death changed me and my life. I naively thought that it would not be difficult to put this story down on paper.

I thought, "I've mourned, I've dealt with the grief and am a very happy person, so blessed with a wonderful life, so it will be simple." I could not have been more wrong. It was very difficult to relive my teenage grief as I wrote. But like all things in life that are really hard, I've learned from writing her story.

I now understand that grief is life-long. It changes, but it's always there. Some years nearer the surface than others, but never gone. Some years and days, greater in intensity than others, but never gone. Those that say you "get over it" are wrong, I believe. A loss, any time in life, but especially of a parent as a child, is always a part of you, a part of the fabric of a person. I did "get over" the crying and sadness, the mourning part of grief, in time, but not over my grief for her. I never will, and that's ok. Grief is a lifelong learning process.

During my consulting career, I traveled extensively. One of the companies I worked for had a facility in Krakow, Poland. I was sent to help set up a new office there and took the time to visit Auschwitz, the Nazi death camp that is a few hours from Krakow.

On the tour, I was overwhelmed by the pain that still engulfs this place. The entire camp is full of horrifying reminders of the death that happened there, but the one that impacted me the most was a huge room of shoes - thousands, of all sorts - that had been left by those who were gassed. The sight of this room hit me like a punch to the gut. All of these people's shoes, from infants to grandparents, baby's first walking shoes to sole barren work boots. Their pain, their grief was unthinkable. It made me think that my pain from Mom's death, which sometimes consumed me, was just so small in comparison to that which others had endured. My tears, while real and not to be downplayed, were like a little drop of water in the ocean of tears that others had cried. It made me more grateful for my wonderful life and mindful of other's sorrows.

My Mom's death changed me and my siblings (you will read about their individual experience with her death and our Dad's death in the chapters that follow) in ways that shaped who we are now.

Writing these words made me so grateful for that change. I like to think I'm a better person for having had this struggle - with her death, with Him, with who I want to be. If she'd lived, I may have had a much easier life (or perhaps not; we'll never know), but I'd be different.

Mom
By Ellen Krohne

Written in July 2013, shortly after Bill and I had our first two grandchildren, Lincoln and Bill.

I wonder who my Mom would be
If she had lived as long as me

She left us when she was so young
Seven little ones, so much undone

Her leaving changed us in many ways
To live for today, to learn to pray

Was she happy? I don't know
Sometimes she let her sadness show

She never felt that grandchild bliss
That "light up" smile, a butterfly kiss

I wear yellow to keep her close
Helps to make up for the ache of loss

Ellen Krohne

My life I've lived to make her proud
Some days I've heard her laugh out loud

I pray now that she feels our love
And keeps sending blessings from above

Photographic Interlude

Delores Ann Mueller at age 22, as a bridesmaid at her sister Eleanor's wedding. This photo is also on Mom's tombstone.

The photo on the front cover of the book is taken in our back yard of Mom as she laughed and ran away from the camera – she hated having her photo taken. It's always been one of my favorite photos of her.

The photo on the back cover is one of the hundreds of pictures of Dad, Mom and Gary as a baby.

Dad as a young man, prior to their getting married, standing proudly by his farm truck "A. H. Mueller Lenzburg, IL" probably around his 21st birthday.

Mom and Dad on their wedding day in Grandma Mueller's yard.

This is a photo of our family farm house and farm buildings, taken from Grandma Mueller's front yard.

The only picture we have of all seven of us as kids, taken at Ann's First Communion in 1963. Gary, 10 years old, on the far left is holding Dan who is four months old. In front of him is Betty who is five, I am in the middle of the picture and am seven, Annie is eight, in the white veil next to me. Tom, who was two, is in front of Ann holding the book and Bill, four, is to her left side.

On the first pages of the book is the same photo with Mom and Dad, the only one we have of all of us.

Dan's First Communion photo with Mom and Dad. This was taken in April of 1970, just five months before she died.

School photos from 1970 of the seven of us. Gary was a senior in high school, Annie a sophomore, I was a freshman. Below are Betty, who was in 7th grade, Bill in 5th grade, Tom in 3rd grade and Dan in 2nd. These were taken in mid-September, just before Mom died.

This is the baby quilt that Annie, Betty and I stitched and Grandma Mueller, Aunt Loretta and the three of us quilted for Mom. Baby Robert was wrapped in it at the funeral home visitation. We assumed it had been left in the casket with him. It was found a couple of years ago in a box of quilts that Dan had and it was gifted to me at my 60th birthday party. A Mueller family treasure.

Gary driving the newest tractor we owned with Tom behind him. We had an even older John Deere we called "Putt-Putt." Bill and Dan are sitting pretty on top of the hay bales they just loaded. This was taken in October 1973.

March 1976 at Betty's wedding in the St. Libory Church, Annie and I by her side as her attendants.

Dad and Ardell's wedding at the St. Libory Church in June 1977. Four boys in the back row, Gary, Tom, Bill and Dan. Ardell and Dad in the middle. Front row is me, Betty and Annie.

Dad with all of the grandchildren from the seven of us except Gary's second son, Joe (he was there, must have just missed this picture). Back row from the left; Josiah, Annie's oldest, Tim, Gary's youngest, Nikki, Gary's third, Michael, Gary's oldest, Joy, my oldest, holding Rebecca, Tom's youngest, Luke and Matt, Betty's identical twin boys.

Middle row is Katherine Delores, Dan's oldest, Melanie, Bill's oldest, Rachael, Tom's oldest, Noah, Annie's youngest, and Ab, my youngest. Front row is Spencer, Dan's youngest, Dad, Robbie, Bill's youngest and John, Tom's second. Dad was sure proud of all these fine grandchildren!

Recent photo taken at Aunt Loretta's 75th birthday party in St. Libory. Tony and Delores Mueller's flock from youngest to oldest - from left to right; Dan, Tom, Bill, Betty, Ellen, Annie and Gary.

Part 2

The Siblings Speak, Dad's Final Chapter and Grief Learnings

In Part II, I tell my four brothers' and two sisters' stories of their grief and growing up, one at a time, youngest to oldest. To enable me to voice their stories, I developed 35 interview questions, met with them and spent many hours talking, crying and laughing, and then I wrote their stories from these discussions. (The questionnaire I used is Appendix A). Included in these chapters are other personal details of our family.

Before each of Chapters 10-15 is a short poem that I wrote for that sibling about the experience they related to me for this book.

Chapter 16 is the story of our Dad's struggle with leukemia and his death and how we dealt with his passing. Before Chapter 16 is a poem I penned after I wrote Dad's chapter.

Chapter 17, the last chapter, offers insights from our grief journey, providing some conclusions and thoughts on managing grief that my siblings and I hope are helpful to you, dear reader.

Chapter 10

Dan

He can't bring up her image,
Not her smell or touch
He'll never know
She loved him so much

He has little recollection
of that sad day in September
Dan just cannot recall
He does not remember

Ellen Krohne

I do not remember.

My brother Dan is the youngest sibling, just seven when Mom died. He can't bring up her face, her smile, her eyes. He can't hear her laughter or smell her cooking. He just cannot recall. He doesn't remember how she doted on him and rocked him to sleep. How she kept him in the crib in their bedroom long after he was old enough to be in a regular bed, because she liked having her baby there with her. He doesn't remember how she'd laugh at the precious antics of her littlest child; a little blonde-haired, blue-eyed cutie, so sweet he'd melt your heart. He was able to get away with a lot, as this "baby" belonged to all of us.

Most of what he knows of Mom, his "picture of her," is from the stories he has heard about her from us. The stories of her sense of humor, her love of gardening and her great cooking.

One of his handful of memories of her is a distraction. He was sitting at the east window of the kitchen on her lap as she was taking a splinter out of his hand. It seemed she did that a lot, as splinters are a way of life for kids on a farm. Mom said "Danny, do you see that pretty flower outside?" While he looked for it, she cut open his hand and removed the splinter. He remembers it was a pretty flower.

At the top of the stairs between the girls' and boys' bedrooms was a landing. There was always a large grey metal trash can with a lid on this landing, with a 30-gallon bag of flour inside. "Go upstairs and get me a cup of flour, Danny," Mom would instruct her youngest several times a day as she baked. "And don't spill it." Dan would proudly deliver the flour to Mom.

He remembers that we would work all afternoon on an outdoor "performance" for Mom and sometimes Dad would watch too. Dan liked putting on a circus best of all. We'd drape a sheet over the clothesline poles as a backdrop for our circus. Ann was always the ringmaster, announcing all the acts. Betty would tightrope-walk across some bricks that had been set in a row. Bill would perform some feat of strength, like lifting a heavy barbell made from straw. Tom and Dan were always the circus animals – first elephants, then lions, tigers, and horses - such simple fun.

Mom was an expert at toilet training by the time Dan was ready. She was also busier than imaginable with all seven of us and the work around the farm. When Dan was training he'd be set on the toilet. When he was done, he'd call to Mom, "I am done," softly at first, then gaining momentum as no one arrived, until finally he was yelling at the top of his lungs, "I AM DONE," before someone would come to rescue him. The "I AM DONE" phrase still brings a laugh when we tease him now.

He has almost no memories of her death; just one scene at the church during her funeral. At Mom's funeral Mass, he remembers walking back and forth on the kneeler, wondering what we were doing there. Aunt Loretta told him to sit down and behave, because this was important. He didn't realize it was Mom in that casket.

Dan's first memory of missing Mom was sometime in the first year she was gone, when he realized she was not there because of his stomach – he was hungry. There was no dinner and not much to eat in the house. Mom never let this happen – where was she?

"He lost his center, his base, his grounding," is how Dan describes Dad in those years after Mom died. "He flamed out, and that had a big ripple effect on all of us." Without Mom there, Dad didn't seem to have control and Dan wished Mom would have been there to stop him. To stop him from starting the day with the blackberry brandy shots and from spending his days in the tavern. To stop him from wasting his money buying a bar in Bartelso, a nearby town in Clinton County.

Dan remembers Dad bringing home a "housekeeper," Julie, when he was about 12 years old. She was an older woman, a bartender at the bar in Bartelso. She lived with Dad and the boys for a while, taking the bedroom in the back of the house in which we'd all slept before Dad finished the upstairs bedrooms. She was there to help with the cooking and cleaning. As Dan describes it, she didn't spend much time at either of these, but at least someone was there. She smoked and made the house smell horrible. At least Dad never had that habit.

Dad got aggravated with Julie for not cooking enough for the boys; they were still growing and were virtual eating machines. Julie enlisted Dan's help to make a massive batch of fresh chicken salad. Dan pulled the fresh chicken meat off of the bones, sending chicken grease everywhere. Julie ground up the meat and added eggs, celery, pickles and mayonnaise. There were containers of the stuff all over the house. Dan loved it, as there was plenty to eat for weeks. He still smiles when he thinks about their chicken salad-making mess!

Julie died shortly after that and her children came and took her belongings from our house. Somehow Dad had the title to her 1965 Dodge Coronet. Dan drove that car when he turned 16. The last sibling was the only one that didn't have to buy his own car before getting his license. At least that was a little something for Dan.

Soon after Julie died, Dad met Ardell, a widow from Waterloo, Illinois who had five children, four grown and one, Mike, still at home. It was August 1976. Uncle Harold asked if he could bring Ardell to my wedding and I said sure. Uncle Harold had been married to Dad's sister, Marie, who had passed away a few years earlier. Uncle Harold had remarried recently to Ruth, and Ardell was a friend of hers. Dad and Ardell dated and then married the next year, in June of 1977.

A widow and widower had remarried and together they had a total of 12 children. Mom's magic number.

"She saved him. Dad had focus and purpose again. He had a helper, a partner again. I was so glad they got married," Dan said. She kept Dad in check, providing that level of control that he needed. She was also there to cook and to help Dan with homework. She was a savior to both Dad and Dan.

After Ardell came, there was to be no more talk of Delores. "I have a husband dead and buried in Waterloo, and we're not talking about him, so no need to talk about Delores," she said once. Dan's thoughts and memories of Mom waned even more with a stepmother in the house. Only after Dad died did he think more of his mom, Delores.

As he did remember Mom more, he wasn't angry or upset like many of his older siblings – he realized by then that there was nothing he could do about her being gone. Mom had a strong influence on his life, though. When he grew up, he sought a strong, independent thinker for his wife. Dan strongly values women's rights and believes that a woman should be independent, not having a man tell her what to do. Especially on abortion. "If Mom would have chosen that path, we would not have lost her," Dan stated flatly.

Dan is certain that the experience of losing Mom at such a young age influenced him to be compassionate and caring to others in his life, especially family. We seven siblings banded together and cared for each other. He is proud that we made it together.

Dan feels that if Mom had lived we wouldn't have lost the family farm. Losing our family's legacy in farming is heartbreaking to him. Perhaps it wouldn't be a big farm, maybe it would be a specialty farm instead of a grain farm. But the family farm was sold in 1987 and after that we drifted away from Mom's family, the Schmersahl's and our farming roots. Mom wouldn't have let that happen.

Dad sold the last 20 acres of farmland and our family farmhouse when he retired in 1987 and decided to move "to town." Dad and Ardell moved to Waterloo to the home that she had been renting to her son and his family during the years she lived on our farm. The last vestige of our family heritage is now just three acres and the original farmhouse where Grandma and Loretta lived. When Loretta died in 2015, our sister Ann and her husband, Jim, bought that farmstead and are in the process of remodeling the house and moving there. At least the home place is not out of the family yet.

Dan knows of Mom's love for gardening and growing things through others' stories and memories. He is the one in the family that carried on her love of trees, plants and the soil. Dan graduated from the University of Illinois with a degree in Agronomy and has made his career working near the land for the USDA and then at the Gardens at Southern Illinois University in Edwardsville. He's the family expert and helps us all lovingly tend to our trees and properties.

In 2012, the seven siblings placed a beautiful picnic bench in the Gardens at Southern Illinois University in honor of Mom. Mom's love of gardening, education, and cooking came together well in this memorial in a university garden. It was Dan that made all the arrangements and had the plaque, which read, "In loving memory of Delores Mueller," placed at the dedication.

All seven of us married and had children, with five of us having daughters. Dan is the only one to honor Mom in a most special way. His daughter bears her name, Katherine Delores Mueller. She bears a striking resemblance to her grandmother, is a strong independent woman, and she loves to read.

Mom would be so proud.

Chapter 11

Tom

I'll never laugh
I'll never smile
Consumed with sadness
Just a nine-year-old child

But Tom now laughs
Is happy most days
Because "I said so"
He heard God say

Dad was unhappy about something Dan had done, saying, "He just doesn't have a full load. Gary, he has a full load of chromosomes, Bill has the next most, then Tom. And poor Dan, he just doesn't have many."

"What about the girls?" Tom asked.

At Dad's reply, "Girls don't have chromosomes," Tom could not help but laugh.

"That's the most stupid thing I've ever heard you say, Dad."

"Well, dammit, it's true!" That was Dad's typical response. He was right even when all logic pointed to him being wrong.

I couldn't help but add the chromosome story again. It's on the first pages of this book, if it sounds familiar, but it is one of Tom's favorite memories of growing up with Dad. Tom is the second-youngest of the seven of us. Of all the siblings, he and I look the most alike, with brown hair and dark brown eyes and skin that tans at the first peek of sun.

He also shares my inability to throw up, although in his case the problem was not nun induced. It was because Mom once instructed Tom, "Be a good boy and don't throw up in church." To this day, he cannot throw up. We are close, and it feels like we always have been.

Tom is our son, Ab's, godfather. Being a godparent in the Catholic church is an important responsibility. The godparent promises to help raise up the child in His ways, to provide spiritual guardianship and a living example of faith throughout their lives. We trusted Tom to take this responsibility seriously and he has.

Tom is the family's storyteller, a role he relishes, and he has worked to hone his skills. Maybe it's because he lives far from all of us, in Knoxville, Tennessee and has for 30 years. He's raised his family farther away from home than the rest of us, but kept us all vibrantly alive to his three children through relaying the family stories.

Stories about our childhood and the simple fun we had; stories about silly things we said and did, before and after Mom died. When he and his wife and family come back to Illinois, we all get together and laugh and correct each other's versions of the stories.

For example, the three little boys used to play Monopoly for hours on end. Bill always won, and he was always the banker. Tom and Dan suspected that he hid a $500 bill under the game board, which Bill denied adamantly. But they always let him be the banker, anyway.

Another favorite story comes from a lazy Sunday afternoon when we were all watching TV together. First, we watched a car chase where the bad guys were stopped by the police shooting out the tires. Next, we watched one of those action-packed Westerns. The covered wagon was out of control, heading to the cliff, I jumped up and shouted, "Shoot for the tires, shoot for the tires!" My brothers and sisters rolled on the floor laughing. That one's told every time we get together.

Tom's three children most enjoy the story about their dad's Halloween adventure. He was a teenager and needed a costume to wear to a school function. I dressed him up as a girl, pantyhose and all. He thought someone was messing with his leg when he got a runner in the pantyhose! My motive was not very pure, though. I thought it was good for all boys to have to wear makeup, a bra, pantyhose, skirt and heels for a day, so they would know how uncomfortable all that feels. He sure was a cutie as a girl!

Tom has a few more memories of Mom than Dan does (well, his extra chromosomes probably help that, right?) He remembers the genuine affection she had for all of us, including him. He remembers how much he enjoyed spending time with her, when she had it to spare in her hectic day.

"The morning after she went to the hospital to have the baby, I remember hearing wailing and screaming and running down the stairs as fast as I dared. There never were any handrails on those steep stairs. I remember not understanding what was going on. You all were sitting around crying, screaming, 'Mom's dead. Mom's gone.' I was in shock. It couldn't be true, couldn't be happening. I tried to pretend it wasn't true. That didn't work; she was still gone."

"I don't remember anything of the next day, until we were at Moll Funeral Home for the visitation. We had to stand in that receiving line. Dad was first, then all of us kids. I was crying. There were so many people, they just kept coming and I just kept crying. Streams of people. I don't remember anyone trying to comfort me. I was just standing there crying. Betty, I think it was Betty, leaned over and said, 'Stop it, stop crying right now,'" Tom remembers vividly.

"I remember standing in that line with my Mom behind me, lying in that casket, and I was feeling lost and so scared. Uncertain of so many things. Like, who is going to cook me breakfast and get me to school? Who will wash my clothes and help me with homework? Mom did everything. Dad didn't do anything for us. I was so confused about how we were going to make it. I was so scared."

Tom remembers walking up the long middle aisle to the first pew at St. Libory Church the morning Mom was buried. The whole church was full: all the school kids were there and it seemed most of the town. "I was embarrassed crying in front of my classmates," he recalls. "But I couldn't stop." He doesn't remember anything else from the funeral.

His eyes filled with tears as he recalled his most vivid memory of his entire childhood. "We got home from the funeral. It was a gorgeous September afternoon, sunny with a little breeze, just a perfect fall day in the country. I went to the back yard by myself and started walking, thinking, 'I'll never laugh again, I'll never smile again.' Swearing that to myself over and over."

Nothing but sadness ahead for this little, nine-year-old boy.

And Tom remembers the tremendous sorrow in the little farmhouse. Sadness where before there was yelling and arguing between Mom and Dad. He hated that arguing at the time, but longed for it compared to this feeling. Dad was drinking even more, coping the best he could.

Soon after Mom was gone, Dad had to learn to manage the house. Tom remembers Dad doing so much more than before, cooking especially. Good thing it was going into winter, when he was typically laid off from his construction job. Dad had to learn to grocery shop, something he'd never done. Tom recalls that Dad would bring home the same things repeatedly, things that we didn't eat, like pork and beans. He'd buy four cans of them, and we hadn't touched the 24 cans he'd bought in weeks prior.

Then, he figured it out; just buy cases of Cap'n Crunch cereal and milk and it would work out. "I still love that sweet treat, even after eating it for all those years. But, you have to prepare it just right – soak it for several minutes in milk before diving in – that preparation is important or you could break a tooth," Tom says with a smile.

Tom coped with his grief by rocking, which had been his go-to calming behavior since he was little. He'd rock and just sit and think in this little wooden rocking chair we had in the living room or in the one upstairs in the boys' bedroom. Tom smiles as he recalls another of the favorite family stories.

"You remember, Ellen, the time when you had read somewhere about the symptoms of the disease called autism and because I rocked all the time, you thought I might be autistic. I said, 'No, no, I am not autistic. I can't draw, can't paint, or nothing like that!'" We still laugh at that one!

As it turns out Tom was just good at settling himself through his rocking. He took long walks around the farm alone and read a lot too. He cried privately and lost himself in daydreams. All these things helped ease his grief. Tom felt badly for his brother Bill, and still does. "Mom being buried on his birthday, Bill got the worst of the deal."

Tom's classmates were understanding. "Mostly I think they were extra nice to me because they were glad this hadn't happened to them." Once when a lawn mower was stuck in the school yard, Tom and his classmates went and gave it a push to help get it out. Tom got splattered with mud and started crying, sobbing, thinking, "Who's going to wash my clothes now? I'm a mess and Mom's not here to do it." His buddies helped him back into the classroom and "covered" for him when reading started, kindly skipping his turn.

Little gestures like that mean a lot to a grieving child.

There was a nun who was his teacher the year Mom died. "I am pretty sure she is burning in hell right now," Tom said with not a glimpse of a smile. "If not, I think she should be. She was the most non-compassionate person I've ever encountered. I'd be reminded of Mom somehow and start crying in class. She'd yell 'Stop crying, Tom. Stop that now.'"

Tom remembers that at Mother's Day that year his teacher was especially mean. All the kids were making a gift for their mother in class. Tom told her he wasn't going to, he didn't have a mother any more. She didn't care. She insisted he do the project anyway and when he refused she got very angry. "Just give it to your grandmother," the nun said. But Tom didn't make that project. He is stubborn when proving a point that he knows is right. Like Dad in that regard.

Tom remembers the discussions about the seven children being split up, going to our godparents' homes, perhaps. He says maybe we should have been separated, given how bad things were at home.

Tom smiles as he says, "I would have been fine with that, with going to either one. One of the greatest blessings Mom and Dad gave me was my godparents; they were the best godparents! Aunt Eleanor, she has this contagious enthusiasm, always sure everything will be okay. Uncle Claude is the person I'm named for, Thomas Claude. When I was little the kids nicknamed me 'Dirt Clod,' making fun of my middle name. I didn't care. I was proud to be named for him. He was a great role model; a good provider, husband and father. He was a steadying influence for me. He always gave me such cool gifts too. I decided as I grew into adulthood that I wanted to be just like Uncle Claude."

As the months went by after Mom's death, Tom didn't cry as much. He internalized his grief. He didn't talk about it or express his feelings openly. That was what was expected of us strong German folks, the conventional view of what to do: get over it.

Tom didn't carry that conventional wisdom with him into adulthood. He made the conscious decision to express his emotions, to show his love and say,

"I love you." He ends every phone call I've had with him all these years with the words "love you." A conscious decision to not take a chance that we won't speak again and he's not said it. His normal attitude is "I cry, I express my emotions. People that know me well know and respect that I'm emotional."

Losing Mom made him very aware that he should not take those he loves for granted. It was a purposeful and pivotal decision in his life. His wife, Sara and three children, those beautiful children he purposefully brought into this world, he doesn't take for granted that they will be there. "I may disagree vehemently with them, and express that too, but will never take them or their love for granted," Tom emphatically states. "Because I realize they can be gone at any time, not by their choice."

"I didn't even get to say goodbye to Mom. The night she went to the hospital, she said to me, 'I'll be back in a few days with the new baby.' We didn't hug or say I love you; she was just gone."

Tom made other conscious changes in his life too. Being the son of an alcoholic, he has been witness to its impact. "My father started and ended every day with a drink. I knew I was never going to do that. The cost to our family was immense. Not just in Dad's health, or that Mom and he argued about his drinking, or his lack of ability to parent us, but the economic cost too. Our family could have had so much more if Dad didn't drink. So, I made the decision to be a change agent for the generation. Assuming I'm predisposed to alcoholism, I decided I would abstain. I wanted to be sure my children knew not to drink, that alcohol is dangerous. That lesson was important for me to impart to them."

"Another important lesson is that in spite of all of this, the seven Mueller children not only survived, but thrived. We made it against the odds that we wouldn't."

Tom thinks of the farm and Dad's life from a different perspective too - an economic one. Probably his mindset and experience as a Professor of Agriculture at the University of Tennessee shining through. "Dad spent so much time and energy supporting his mother, Mary Mueller, and her farm, that the Tony and Delores Mueller farm didn't thrive. He didn't buy more ground to turn his farm into 200 or 300 acres, like all the other farmers around us did. From a farm economics perspective, that was a fatal mistake. Instead, he farmed his Mother's ground until she died, and then it was sold to a neighboring landowner. He grew a family, but didn't prosper financially, selling parts of his small farm as he couldn't keep up with the bills over the years."

Tom is the opposite of Dad in that regard too. He looks wistfully as we discuss what Mom would think of his life today. "She'd say, 'Oh, Tommy, you did so well!' She'd be proud that I have a Ph.D. and am respected as a professional in the weed science industry, traveling all over the globe to speak on papers I author. She'd love my house, be so proud of my beautiful and supportive wife, Sara.

She'd love that Sara is such a good mother, staying home to take care of the children until they were in school. Of course, Mom would have expected me to convert her to a Catholic. On the other hand, I may never have met Sara, as Mom would probably not have wanted me to go out of state for school. If she would not have died, that surely would have changed my life, but we'll never know in what ways."

"She was sure set on us all going to college, though. She pushed us all and praised us too. The expectation for A's was strongly instilled early in our lives. Even as a nine-year-old, I can still hear her saying, 'You are smart and it is expected that you will make good grades. You should be getting A's.' I passed that on to my children too. A is for Adequate," Tom said.

"Dad's advice was a little different, though. I went to college at your insistence, Ellen, and when I left, his only words of advice for me were, 'Keep it in your pants, son.'" Tom and I laughed for a while at that one.

Tom knows Mom wanted more in life. "She was very materialistic; she wanted and envied all those things others had that we didn't. She wanted us all to 'make something of ourselves, so we could buy those things, have the status she didn't,'" Tom remembers. He has worked hard to do just that.

Years after they were married, Tom sought help with his grief at Sara's insistence. He went to see a counselor when he found himself, again, in a general "funk" in the fall. In talking to the counselor, he came to understand that he was very normally grieving his mother's death anniversary. The counselor helped him realize his malaise didn't change anything and helped him to realize he was just very normal in his grieving her loss.

Tom was also struggling with his faith. Decades after Mom's death, the unresolved question lingered, "Why? How can a loving God kill my Mother? I was really struggling, praying, seeking an answer. I was driving to Raleigh, North Carolina, to see a friend, John, who was dying.

John said, 'You didn't drive six hours to ask me how I am doing. What do you really want to know?'"

Tom said, "I want to know spiritually, are you okay?"

John assured me he was, 'I'm good.'"

"I was working through my friend's impending death, and my question to God about Mom burned brightly as I drove home, talking to God, struggling mightily. 'I want an answer,' I said to myself. 'Why did you kill my mom?' I was on I-40 westbound outside of Statesboro, North Carolina, in the heart of the Bible Belt. There are lots of billboards on those roads. As I drove on the interstate, one came into my vision. It was a black one with white letters that shone brightly:

"BECAUSE I SAID SO."
GOD

"It hit me like a brick to the head. I'd never seen this billboard anywhere before and have not seen it ever again. It was His message to me, directly to me, the answer I'd been struggling to find. "I AM THE GOD WHO KNOWS EVERYTHING, I KNOW MORE THAN YOU, I AM IN AUTHORITY AS I HAVE THE POWER TO BE. **BECAUSE I SAID SO**, THAT IS WHY, Tom."

"I realize to some people this may seem to be a wholly unacceptable answer to my question. But I felt unbelievable peace, unbelievable solace in this answer. I've not questioned Him on Why again. His answer gave absolute closure to my grief. As nonsensical as that sounds, it is absolutely true for me," Tom cried as he relived this testament of God's love for him.

Tom and his family are strong Evangelical Charismatic Christians. He demonstrates his religious belief and is active in their church family. Mom may not have liked his choice to leave the Catholic church, but she would love and laugh with the man Dr. Thomas Claude Mueller has become.

Chapter 12

Bill

We buried Mom
On Bill's birthday
Not much sadder
Thing to say

His anger consumed him
For many years
Till Jesus came back to him
Through his tears

"I was angry, so angry, every day from the day she died, just before my 11th birthday, until I turned 16!" was Bill's first recollection of Mom's death. He worked hard to bury that burning anger.

I knew he wasn't the same happy-go-lucky little boy that talked to everyone about everything. The one whose curiosity with the world was only matched by his ability to talk his way out of the blame for mischief he'd started.

After she was gone, he was distant. I didn't understand the depth of his anger until many years later, as we talked about this book. Bill hid that anger, buried it deep down inside where it stewed for years.

Bill didn't cry. I remember all of us crying at the funeral, but Bill knows he didn't. He was too mad; the situation was too out of control. He could control whether he cried or not, so he just bottled up all those tears. He towed that stoic German line. He wasn't crying. Period.

He does remember Mom. Her smile when she was happy; her joy in seeing a child read and enjoy books; trips to the library with her, her desire for her children to go farther in school than she did.

He remembers the day he got his biggest whipping from her, when he was eight or nine years old. Mom wasn't shy about being sure we were all appropriately disciplined. No "Wait till your father gets home," she took matters into her own hands to be sure her children were well-behaved and knew right from wrong.

I felt lucky Mom picked me this time to go with her to pick up some meat at Wenneman's Meat Market in St. Libory. It was a warm spring day, humid and windy, the perfect conditions for a storm. And in southwestern Illinois, spring is tornado season. The storm had come up suddenly. Branches and debris were flying by us but Mom was determined to get home as the rest of the kids were home alone. As we flew down the road the wind was gusting so strongly that she was having trouble keeping the car on the road. Her eyes were wild with fear, and her hands shook on the steering wheel.

When we finally blew into the driveway, the tornado had just passed by our house. The chicken shed that stood just east of the house was gone. The rickety wooden back porch of our farmhouse was strewn across the field between our house and Grandma's. Standing there looking up by the front door stood Bill, mesmerized by the storm and excited about what he'd just seen. The eye of a tornado. A clear circle of sky appeared in its center as the half-formed tornado passed directly overhead. It's a sight few ever live to tell about.

Mom tore into him as she hugged him close. "You could have been killed, what are you doing up here?" Gary had everyone else in the basement, but Bill just wouldn't come in from watching that storm. Bill got the whipping of his lifetime for that insolence, and, thankfully, lived to remember it.

He remembers her cooking too. There were coffee cakes with cinnamon and sugar, so sweet and warm from the oven on bread baking day. Chicken, freshly butchered she fried in hot lard in her big electric skillet, root beer floats with popcorn which we enjoyed as we watched the *Wonderful World of Disney* as a family. Her cherry pie, so fresh and the crust just perfectly flaky. Comfort foods that carry him through times of sadness or stress to this day. When he was a young attorney and working those 70+ hour weeks, he'd sometimes come home famished on a Friday night and eat an entire pie. Comfort foods can be important nourishment to a soul.

He remembers helping Mom cook jelly and ketchup. Mom could get you to stand all afternoon stirring the pot of boiling liquid and thinking it was a reward to be helping her. She had that ability to get us to do things and make them fun. Like her garden, which was just huge every year and grew as her children's appetites grew.

The three boys were in charge of watering it in the dry summer evenings. Bill devised an "artesian drainage system." Really, he just cut trenches between the rows and we'd use them to flood the rows with water. It worked great and was much easier than carrying buckets or watering each plant. Bill was good at figuring things out, always curious why things worked the way they did.

It may have been that curiosity, that constant search for a "Why?" that made him so angry after we lost her.

"The baby's not moving, something's not right," Mom said to Dad. Bill remembers overhearing that conversation a few days before she went into the hospital. Mom had been crying.

He remembers Mom saying to the little boys as she waved goodbye "I love you guys." Ever since then, he has great trouble saying those words to anyone, even now. He loves people deeply, but it is just so difficult for him to get those three words out. The last ones he remembers her saying.

He remembers Dad's words the morning that she died: "Mom's dead, baby, too." To the point and nothing else and Dad went out the door with Gary. Bill doesn't remember much after that, not of the funeral nor the days that followed.

He remembers lots of food and people in the house the first day. Then he remembers nothing about the rest of the week except how angry he was. And remembers bottling up and shutting down. Mad at God and at Dad. At God because he killed her, his mother. Where was He when she needed him? He got so mad at God that he stopped believing in Him altogether.

Deep in his heart, Bill was a functional atheist for many years. He hid that. He was an altar boy, right there with the parish priest, like all the good little boys in St. Libory. He went through confirmation because he had to. All the while he was thinking, "This is crap, there is no God, because if there was she'd still be alive. God was not there when we needed him, so he must not exist."

He remembers going to church after her death and thinking, "What hypocrisy, for us to go to this place and pray to this God. There is no justice in this. Where were you when she needed you? If you were real, you would not have let this happen to me, to us."

Dad forced us all to go to church, and for Bill it was torture. People were pointing at and whispering about our sad family, and it just made him angrier. Bill would go through all the normal motions, all the mandatory signs like the sign of the cross, genuflecting, kneeling; but raging inside was the anger in his heart.

Bill was angry at Dad too. Dad got her pregnant and at his tender 11 years Bill rationalized, "He should not have done that. Then she would still be here." It didn't help that Dad didn't manage his grief well at all. He was gone a lot, drank a lot, and didn't help Bill with his struggle with God in any way – he just wasn't there. Mom would have been able to answer Bill's questions; she always did. But Dad did not.

Bill recalls us girls saying to him, "Mom wouldn't be happy with that grade," when he brought home a "B" in the semester after she died. And he remembers, even in his anger, wanting her to be happy with him.

"I can control my grades, I can do well," became Bill's mission. And he did. He was Salutatorian in his class at Okawville High School, even with taking all of the very hard pre-college classes. In college and law school, too, he made those grades for her. He graduated near the top of his class in both. Working hard at school was one thing he could control.

And he could choose to read. He took himself far away from the sadness in our house. He would read to go to another, better place, where no one had died and God didn't let you down. Science fiction was his retreat. We'd put the boys to bed after supper and chores and turn out all of the lights in the upstairs bedroom which the boys shared, leaving on only the single-bulb in the hall between the bedrooms. If Bill cracked the bedroom door slightly, a sliver of light – just enough for reading - would shine on his bed. Many nights he couldn't sleep and stayed up reading until one or two in the morning. It was not unusual for Bill to read four or five books a week.

Bill still has this passion for reading, just like Mom did. He remembers going to the library with her as a reward for being good. Mom saying, "Read, and you will become something." She wanted us all to do better than she and Dad had done, to get an education and have a great career, to "be something, somebody."

Bill had been with Mom at the Marissa Public Library so often that even after her death, they still let him check out books. He'd beg Aunt Loretta to drive him there, and every couple of weeks she would. For years, they'd give him the first option to shop the night before the opening of their annual book sale. He remembers the kindness of those librarians fondly, and he still has many books in his collection with the "Marissa Public Library" stamp on the bottom of them.

By the time he left home for college, he had hundreds of books. When he ran out of money in college during his first semester, he sold some of his prized books in order to stay in school. After law school, Bill spent years tracking down those titles to buy them back into his collection. He now has a room in his basement that contains his collection, some 2,700 books that he spent almost 50 years assembling.

The 28th of September was the day we buried Mom, and it was Bill's 11th birthday. Bill remembers that every year Dad would go on a drinking binge around the anniversary of her death. There was no acknowledgment that all of his children needed him to be there for them. We were all saddest on her death anniversary days each year, but for Dad, Bill's birthday became the day of mourning for Mom, not celebrating for Bill.

"The positive thing that did come from Mom's death and Dad's lack of nurturing us through our grief was to make the seven of us strong together. We had to pull together to make it," Bill remembers. "After Mom's death, the house was often far less than clean, but if we found out that someone was coming over, we all pulled together and got things 'presentable.' In part, it was a matter of pride that we could do so, but in part, there was always a fear that we would be separated. We could condense weeks of cleaning into hours, and many seemed amazed at how orderly the house was, even without a mother to take care of things."

"Those days made us stronger as a unit," Bill recalls. "We would do anything for another member of the family and take on all comers who would challenge any one of us. As a family, we did not always agree; in fact, agreement was pretty rare on many topics, even now when we are adults, but one thing was true. We were family. Family comes first and you do all you can for family."

Bill remembers the three boys, he, Tom and Dan, were on their own a lot. They would just take off for the day on the farm. They might dam up a creek or dig a tunnel in a field. Maybe they'd make a fort in the pasture and spend the day there reading. He remembers not having good things to eat – just peanut butter and the Cap'n Crunch cereal that Dad would buy in cases. He still can't eat those foods to this day.

It's amazing given this less than nutritious diet, but Bill grew like a weed between seventh and eighth grade. He was six feet tall, thin and strong, like the pictures of Dad as a youth. The basketball coach at St. Libory Grade School asked Bill to join the basketball team. There were two other tall boys in the class, and the coach saw the potential of a winning season if Bill could also play on the team.

Dad never saw the value in sports or extracurricular activities. They just kept you away from doing the farm chores. Dad didn't see the value in education past high school, either: it was just a big waste of money. His views were so very different than Mom's. But Bill was convincing, and he could make a good argument for almost anything, even as a child. Dad finally relented and said that Bill could join the team.

Bill played and the team did great, going 24-0 in the regular season and did not lose until it came up against a very large school from Carbondale. The whole town rooted for the team.

Dad never came to a single game. Most of the time, he didn't make it to the gym to pick Bill up from practice either. The coach would just nod when Bill was the last one there to be picked up and take Bill home himself. Never a bad word said, just a good example set by that kind coach.

Years later when Bill had two children that were both active in sports and activities, he made almost every practice and did not miss a game. He was there for them. In life, we either become our parents or we do the opposite. Bill's path was clear.

Bill grew up. He did well in school. But Bill was not okay. Anger and sadness permeated his being all the time. He remembers laughing and enjoying things those years after Mom died, but not loving like before. Joyfulness, that kind of joy you have deep in your heart, went with her too. He couldn't love or really be joyful, certainly not toward God and really not toward anyone. That was gone.

Thankfully, that changed.

Lorraine Weber was a dear friend of Mom's. Lorraine and Vernon's children were a little bit younger than we were. I babysat them often. We lived just a few miles apart. Lorraine had become very active in a new movement in the Catholic church called Teens Encounter Christ (TEC). TEC was a retreat that Catholic teenagers attended to deepen their faith and ability to pray. It was set up as a long weekend, Friday evening to Sunday afternoon. Adults like Lorraine assisted with the retreats, but the teens that had attended a TEC before actually led them.

She asked Bill several times to attend a TEC, but he resisted. He saw no reason to go to a prayerful retreat, as there was no God. Not that he told Lorraine that. He used a valid excuse; he was working as a busboy at the Original Mineral Springs Hotel in Okawville, and his shifts were on weekends. He was baling hay, too, for neighboring farmers. He especially enjoyed working for good friends of Mom's, Alice and Victor Shubert. They worked him hard, fed him well, and paid him well. Bill was saving up for college, which he knew Dad would not fund.

Lorraine persisted in her desire for Bill to attend a TEC. Every time she saw him she told him that she was praying for him to attend.

Bill finally relented when he was 16, now a junior at Okawville High School, and agreed to attend, mostly to get Lorraine to leave him alone. He expected to encounter a big NOTHING on this Teens Encounter Christ retreat. To Bill, God was nothing, Christ was non-existent. The contempt in his heart would not change. He'd go through the motions, just like at church.

Each TEC had a title, based on the town in which it was held and on the number of TEC's that had been held there previously. Bill's first TEC was Sparta 17, held in Sparta, Illinois, just an hour's drive from St. Libory.

At the TEC the teens gave the talks, and the first evening's talks focused on the concept that bad things do happen to good people, but through this we become stronger. The TEC participants were all boys around the same age. As the evening progressed, a service began in the chapel. It was very dark, there were lots of candles in the chapel. The priest made his way to the altar and put a consecrated host in a monstrance and informed us that Christ was present in our midst. The boys were all in a circle around that altar with locked arms and were encouraged to pray what was in their hearts and to talk to God.

Bill hadn't prayed in years. There had been no reason and no belief in any prayer that had been said in all those years. But this was different. Perhaps it was the talks of the day. Perhaps it was the support of those around him, encouraging him to "Let it out" and "Just speak to God." So he did. It started out softly, but eventually the dam, built up over the years of holding back his emotions, broke down and Bill began to speak from his heart how he felt.

As Bill opened his heart to God and to this group, out spilled all of the anger. "God, you let me down – if you were real you wouldn't have." All the anger, all the dark feeling poured out as he prayed his feelings about Mom's death. Bill may have expected nothing to occur, but fortunately something very special happened.

Bill felt God come down to him saying, "It's okay." "Even if you did not believe in me, I still believed in you," and "I am here for you and I always have been." He felt Mom was there too, calming him, and helping him to let go. He could feel her and feel love.

And he believed again.

He decided that it was wrong for him to have blamed God for the events of that September morning. He heard the message of those wonderful teen speakers, and he had a renewal of his faith. And when he made that decision to accept Jesus again into his heart and forgive God for Mom's death, he felt an amazing peace come over him... for the first time in years. And he started crying.

He started crying in the middle of that group of young teens standing before an altar, and he didn't stop. He cried all night, and the teen leaders stayed with him. It was an extreme release of emotion. For the first time in years he felt joyful, loving.

For the first time since Mom died.

The change was profound. Bill's faith was back and in many respects, so was he. He felt able to be joyful and happy and laugh again. Gone were the dark days of the past when he had been so angry and mad. He had faith in his heart and the ability to love himself and others.

This is surely why Bill has dedicated so much of his life to these events, serving on over 50 retreats. He was very active in TECs in his youth, then, as an adult was a leader of Koinonia retreats. Eventually, he directed three of the wonderful Koinonia weekends and encouraged others to go as well, leading others in our family, including me, to these healing, powerful experiences.

Once Bill started crying at that first TEC, he's not stopped. Bill is now the big softie in the family, the one who cries at every joyous occasion, Hallmark commercial, and any movie dealing with parents and their children.

And the best thing of all, he met his wife of 35 years, Kathy, at a TEC retreat reunion soon after his first TEC. She has been the best partner in his faith and life journey that Bill could have ever found. Without the pain of those many years, he wouldn't have found her.

Kathy finally gave him that birthday-without-mourning party he deserved all those years. He loves her dearly for it.

Years later, Kathy learned about the priest who was given the duty to tell our Dad that Mom had died that night at Red Bud Catholic Hospital. She was told that he never forgot that awful duty and the sad father of seven who lost his wife and youngest child so suddenly. He prayed for our family every day of his life. His prayers, and the prayers of so many other family members and friends, probably allowed us seven siblings to grow and be strong together. Those prayers mattered for us.

Bill's mission for his future was to be a lawyer. That certainly would make Mom proud. Dad hated lawyers, and he made no bones about that. He also thought college was for rich folks, surely not for his kids. He was certainly not going to help his son become a lawyer. When Bill asked Dad for his financial information to help him secure grants to go to Eastern Illinois University, he said, "No." "No, I don't want you to go, and No, I won't give you any money or any of my financial information for the forms."

Not that Dad had money to give Bill or any of us to go to college. His money management theory was pretty much like his theory of genetics - not rational. "Spend all you have, there will be more," was the way he managed. Dad worked hard on the farm and as a carpenter, but spent more than he had and made investments that just didn't turn out right. Like the bar he bought in Clinton County, one county over from our farm. Fortunately, Ardell reigned in that spending and helped bring stability to the household once they married. But not in time for Bill's college application.

As I've mentioned, Bill is persistent and he was going to college, so he asked the Okawville High School guidance counselor what his options were since Dad wouldn't provide the documentation he needed in order to apply for the grants. The counselor said, "Well, you are 17 and you could file to emancipate yourself." Emancipation meant that Bill would be independent from Dad and could file for grants using just his own income, assuring he'd get them. That's just what Bill did. He filed the appropriate paperwork at the local courthouse, was emancipated, and was eventually funded to get his bachelor's degree - on his own.

Bill worked hard, too, each summer at Centralia Container and for local farmers when he could. He made it, graduating from St. Louis University Law School in 1984 with Kathy by his side. He was the first of us to get his degree and the first to get a post-college degree, his JD, and I could not have been prouder of him!! I'm sure Mom was glowing and shining down her praises too.

When Dad got very ill with leukemia years later, he could not afford the medication he needed. He would not take money from Bill or anyone else - he was still that proud German who didn't take aid no matter what the circumstance. It was Tom who concocted a separate, secret bank account to which many of us contributed so Ardell could pay for the drugs to fight his leukemia. Dad never knew. We all pitched in what we could, and Bill, whose business was doing very well, donated anonymously and generously.

"It has always made me feel good to help others financially. Kathy and I over the years developed a rule to our giving. Whether it was Dad, or someone in the family, or a member of a faith community, assistance was always given on the condition of being anonymous. If we helped someone through another person or a group, the recipient was not allowed to know where the money came from," Bill stated. When they helped Dad, he never knew that they did. That came, in part, from Mom who Bill remembers emphasizing, "We were not 'bad' because we did not have money and those who did were not 'better,' so don't make others feel that way when helping them... just help them."

As you may have surmised, Bill is a self-confessed control freak. He has a need for control, mainly because he spent so many years without control after Mom's death. One reason he became a lawyer is that there are clear rules. Being a lawyer made him that "somebody," making Mom proud. Starting his own firm reinforced his ability to control his family's destiny.

Mom's death shaped Bill's life. In hindsight, it was ultimately shaped in good ways. He was left much more self-reliant, stronger and firm in his desire to excel in the matters he could control, like his grades and doing well in his profession. In that moment as he lived through it on the morning of her death and through the very painful, anger-filled teen years when no one helped him cope, Bill became stronger in his resolve to succeed. He could perhaps have been successful if he had not experienced a renewal of his faith through the TEC, but he is eternally grateful for God's invitation to return to Him that evening at Sparta TEC 17. He's not lost Him again.

Bill summarized it for me: "Now my faith is a part of me, a part of my core being, and I try to live a good, Christian life. I'm not perfect, not by any means. I still face doubts, challenges and times when I falter in living a true Christian life. The difference now is that I have my faith in God and the love of a good wife to help me get through the many challenges that I've faced since that terrible morning in September of 1970. I have something and someone to reach out to in times of trouble, who can help me get through it."

He missed Mom the most when his two children, Melanie and Robert, were born. He grieved anew when they were little, knowing how much Mom would have loved Kathy and cherished being Grandma to their children. Mom would have set a great example for them to love and to work hard. She'd have been proud of what he and Kathy have accomplished and the good, giving person Bill is.

Especially that he's learned to cry.

Chapter 13

Betty

She is the middle of the seven
So innocent and pretty
She grew up on that day
That Mom was gone from Betty

But she is strong,
She has the faith of mighty Abraham
Betty trusts
It was all a part of "His plan"

"I felt like a nuisance to her," Betty sighed. "Mom paid a lot of attention to you when you were little and then not until you got ready to go to high school. These were the times Mom knew she could mold you, shape you. In between, she was just too busy to have much time for us individually. I was looking forward to getting to 8th grade, so she'd focus on me, like she did with you, Ellen, and with Annie. To have meaningful conversations with her, to have her attention. We just never got there."

Betty, whose full name is Elizabeth Geralyn, is my younger sister by almost two years. She was in seventh grade when Mom died and was the youngest of the three girls - the middle child. After her came the three little boys in quick succession. "I was in an odd position – the middle," she said. "Mom hadn't even told me the 'facts of life' yet when she died." Although Mom did have Ann tell Betty about how to handle her period when she started that summer of her 12th year. "It was hurtful that Mom couldn't even take the time to have that important discussion with me."

With blonde hair and blue eyes, Betty was a beautiful little girl. And tiny, not like Ann and me with our size 9 feet. Betty was petite, topping out at five feet three inches when fully grown.

Betty was a whiz at school, excelling especially at math. She figures that if Mom had lived, she'd be a CPA today. She would have gone on to college after high school and would be in a very different place in her life now. I believe Mom would be proud of Betty's persistence to get her bachelor's degree. After many years of night school and working full time, she graduated from college the same year as her twin boys. Her career as an IT project manager is perfect for my organized sister.

She is the one who carries on Mom's love of Christmas, decorating their house from top to bottom each December.

Betty is my sister, but also my forever friend. We have planned so many family parties together: wedding and baby showers, birthday and retirement parties. We have a blast making occasions special. She's good at it too. Betty loves to make craft projects and is very thoughtful to make her generous gifts just right.

When I'm hurting about something, I call her – we are that kind of close. Hers is the name carried on through our daughter, Joy Elizabeth, and Joy's daughter, Quinn Elizabeth. I thought I knew my younger sister inside and out, until we sat down to talk about Mom's death for this chapter. I realize now I didn't.

Betty doesn't remember many details of Mom's death. She took to heart the advice of all those around her to "move on, get over it." That seemed the best way to her. So most of those vivid, hurtful details that some of us have held in our hearts, she just let those go long ago. As we talked, she could only recall a few of them. Of course, she teases, she doesn't have much memory in general.

Dad was at the bottom of the stairs calling for her to get up the morning Mom died. "Kids, come down. We lost them both," Dad gently said. "And that was all he said," Betty recalled. She doesn't remember much else except aunts and uncles gathering throughout the day. She remembers a conversation she overheard that day: "The afterbirth split and a blood clot went to her brain, then to her heart and killed her. I didn't know what an afterbirth was: I was just too young to understand."

At the visitation, she remembers going in first, just Dad and us kids. She remembers the baby at Mom's feet and someone, maybe Dad or maybe Aunt Loretta, moving him to Mom's arms. "Moll Funeral Home was packed; so many people were there, it felt like the whole town came. Everyone was crying, me included. It is such a tiny place, and it was bursting with people."

"At the end of the night Aunt Dorothy took pictures, and one of the other aunts got upset at her doing that." The visitation and funeral were so quick, and she remembers gratefully that we didn't have 2 nights for the visitation. She has no memory of the day of the funeral.

Betty does remember her last conversation with Mom before she went to the hospital. Her labor had started at home on the evening of September 25th and her contractions were getting closer together as Gary came in from the field to take Mom to the hospital. One hit Mom in the kitchen and she winced in pain. "Mom yelled at me meanly, 'What are you looking at?' when I stared at her, not knowing what was happening," Betty recalls. Sadly, those were Mom's last words to her.

After the funeral, she remembers that she and the three little boys, all still in grade school, went back to classes on Wednesday. The high school kids, Gary, Ann and I, got to stay out the whole week. She never did understand why. Was her grief less than ours? She thinks Dad may have thought that littler kids just got over the grief more quickly. Whatever the reason, she remembers they went back to school on Wednesday.

Going back to school was what really changed things for Betty.

She was the oldest of the four Mueller children at St. Libory Grade School, and she was now responsible. Responsible for getting herself and the three little boys on the bus in the morning. Responsible for making sure they were dressed and had their lunches and homework with them. Dad wasn't there in the morning, as he left for work before the bus came.

The high school bus came much earlier, so it was her job to be sure they were on that bus with everything they needed. "I became the responsible adult at 12."

Such a dramatic difference for her. This was always Mom's job – to corral the boys and get them on the bus. To sing happy songs as she drove, setting up the day for positive learning. "Now it fell to me. I had to grow up and be responsible, just like that. Here I was a 12-year-old little girl, I didn't even know where babies came from and now I'm the responsible adult."

Not that the boys acknowledged her new authority or remember that she bore that burden every day. But it changed her from the carefree middle child and little sister, to a parent figure. She worried if things didn't go right in the morning. She was the one that the teachers trusted to bring home important information and the one that sat in on the boys' parent-teacher conferences when Dad didn't make it to them. She transitioned to adulthood quickly. "There was a big gap in my childhood; it was over that Wednesday morning," she states flatly.

Betty worked hard at school and at home. She was the one that really helped Dad the most – doing the laundry and trying hard to keep up with it. She missed Mom's cooking so much - no more regular meals, much less her wonderful desserts and special treats. Dad just wasn't good at grocery shopping or managing a home. She remembers him bringing home odd things to cook, maybe because they were cheap, like chicken necks. And cereal - lots of Cap'n Crunch, the new staple in our morning ritual.

When she got to high school, Betty didn't join clubs or socialize much with friends. She had several close friends and that was enough. She took lots of classes, ready to move on, and get through school as quickly as possible. "I had to be like an adult as a teenager. I wanted to get out and be an adult."

From her freshman year on, she worked a lot with me at the OK Drive-Inn. She took all the shifts she could and she saved her money. By the time she was 15, she had enough saved for a car. Her ticket to independence, she drove it to the driver's license facility herself.

There was a bar in Okawville, The Steam Pipe, for young adults. It served beer and wine only, as in 1973 the law changed the minimum age for beer and wine sales to 19. My husband, Bill, who was my boyfriend then, ran the bar, so 16-year-old Betty often came there with me after work. She met a guy from St. Louis there, Joe. He was nine years her senior, and he fell quickly for her. The summer of her junior year she moved in with him. He lived in St. Louis, far away from our home and her family. She was ready to go, to grow up and be an adult, and that's what the next step was for her – to get married and get a job. No hope for college now, just get out and go on with her adult life.

Dad wasn't around much by this time, and as I said, he was vocal about being glad to get us girls out of the house. When Betty also graduated from high school in the middle of her senior year, Dad signed the papers that allowed his 17-year-old daughter to be married. She looked so beautiful in her Bohemian style dress, with Annie and me by her side as bridesmaids. Just so young.

I'm pretty sure Mom was turning over in her grave that day. "She'd have never allowed me to date anyone that much older than me, no less get married that young, if she were here," Betty emphatically declares. "But Mom wasn't there to stop it."

Betty was very pragmatic about the way she worked through her grief. "I got past it. It was just something that happened in my past. I'd moved on, as we were expected to." When a Mass was said for Mom at St. Libory Church on the first Mother's Day after we lost her, Betty was upset. "It made me feel like, great! We are trying to forget, not call attention to her being gone."

"Her death did define us, though," Betty mused. "Thirty years after Mom died, I was at a funeral in Mascoutah, a town near St. Libory. I was being introduced to some friends of the deceased and making the connection to St. Libory I said my maiden name was Mueller. 'Oh, are you one of those Mueller kids whose Mom died having a baby?' the lady asked. That's how our family was known in the region, as that family whose Mom died in childbirth. Not that any of us let her traumatic death stop us from having babies, thank goodness. But it was how we were known."

As Betty got older, though, and matured, she started questioning - asking God the same simple question as the years progressed: "Why?"

"Why did you take her from us so dramatically? Why did you have my life turn out the way it has?" The question burned more and more for her. "It was in my mid-30's. I was contemplating Why? and had a massive revelation, an "AHA!" moment and it became very clear why Mom died, why all this happened."

It was God's plan.

"It was all in His plan. For Mom to have each of us and to die so traumatically, with so much drama just when she did. It was God's plan for me to grow up so abruptly and to marry Joe. It was ordained so I'd have my twin boys, Matt and Luke, when I did. At the time I was supposed to, according to His plan," she states.

It hits me like a ton of bricks as she talks, so calmly, so absolutely trusting that all of this was God's plan for her life, for all of us. What a wonderful gift, to be so certain. To not be a griever for your whole life. To trust so much in Him, that it's okay. To have that answer to the question and know it's the absolute answer.

I am humbled by her faith.

As she talks about His plan for her, she's not bitter or upset about the past, about Mom's death and Dad's lack of parental guidance. Just accepting that it is His will that these things were to pass and accepting of what He has ahead for her. She's appreciative of the gifts she's been given and sure there were guardian angels that helped and saved her along her path.

Betty did a beautiful devotional on "His Plan for Me" at a Women's Guild meeting at the Troy Friedens United Church of Christ where she and her wonderful second husband, Kevin, now attend. He must also have been in His Plan.

Awesome!

Chapter 14

Ann

The devil, he came that night
And blew through Annie's heart
She felt a cruel, relentless guilt
That would not depart

But there is one that's stronger
He's risen from the tomb
She trusted Him and in His time
He brought our Annie home

Ann finds peace on Grandma Mueller's back porch. She always has. It faces east, and the sun rises over the little creek in the back, where Grandma's garden was for many years. It rose the morning Grandpa Mueller lost his fight with diabetes and six months later when the child he would never know, Loretta, was born to his grieving wife. And it rose on the fateful day in September 1970 that changed the world for Ann and for us all.

The sun rose on many hard, working-all-day days. And happy days too - Easter celebrations and long summer dog days drinking tea on this shady retreat. The porch carries especially good memories for Ann. When she was a little girl, she'd hide out there. As a teen, she'd retreat there from the world and felt safe. Today as she and her husband Jim remodel Grandma Mueller's farmhouse, she finds peace of a special kind on that porch – God is especially with her there.

Ann Geralyn, she was named after our Grandma Anna Schmersahl and St. Gerard. In the Catholic faith, St. Gerard is the patron saint of pregnant women and babies, and Mom so firmly believed in him that his name is the root of several of our middle names, Ann Geralyn, Elizabeth Geralyn and Daniel Gerard. I often wonder where St. Gerard was that fateful night and if she was praying to him at the end.

The family was delighted with the birth of the first granddaughter on Mom's side of the family, but Ann had it tough from the start. Mom had gallbladder surgery soon after Ann was born, so Mom didn't get to care for her newborn. Ann was a very colicky baby and wouldn't nurse, so she was the only one of the seven of us that was bottle fed. This was a failure in Mom's eyes. Ann always felt that Mom just didn't develop that bond that is so important to loving a child, in part because Mom was pregnant with me just four months after giving birth to Ann.

"No, I was not her favorite – I wish I had been. I was her problem child," Ann realizes. "There was nothing I could do to please her. Never. I was the scapegoat for anything that was going wrong. It's amazing I'm at all well-adjusted and functioning, given her verbal abuse of me," Ann sadly laughs.

I remember that Mom's tone and temperament was always different with Ann, exasperated at the start and meaner than with the rest of us. And Ann had a knack for aggravating Mom. Ann believes that because she was so much like Mom, Mom saw all the things she wanted to fix in herself and tried to fix those in Ann. She was chatty as a tween, always talking, always with so much to say about nothing.

Ann had inherited Mom's stubbornness, with no intention of being changed. Ann fought back, and that conflict filled the house, with Dad as the mediator and advocate for Ann. "He was always there for me, the loving influence I needed," Ann remembers of Dad.

This ability to fight back was what would save Ann in the struggle she had ahead; she was strong in spirit.

As Ann grew, she became the family's creative soul, talented in so many ways. She was artistic, had a wonderful singing voice and her dramatic abilities won her the lead in the eighth-grade school play.

And, Ann also had a special gift. All of her life she had a special relationship with God - she had faith in Jesus and felt His presence in her. She was a strong, prayerful Catholic girl, even considering being a nun as she turned 15. She's not sure that, had Mom lived, she would have become a nun, but she definitely knew and was certain about Jesus and his love.

Ann remembers a "truce" of sorts being declared between her and Mom, unspoken of course, but understood, when Mom found out she was pregnant at age 40. Mom had lots of health issues, with varicose veins and thyroid problems, and needed Ann's help to get through the pregnancy. Just preparing the daily meals and getting the household work done was hard on Mom now. Ann was always Mom's right hand in the kitchen, her sous-chef they'd call it now.

Mom wanted the house to look nice when the new baby arrived. This was right up Ann's alley. Together they painted the worn-out linoleum floors. They probably wouldn't have been nearly as worn, except Mom scrubbed them constantly on her hands and knees, like all good German women did in that day. It was imperative to have a clean house. "Cleanliness is next to Godliness," I can still hear her say. Ann felt good to be able to help her now. Maybe she'd do this well for Mom and their relationship would change for the better.

The floors turned out well – colorful and fresh. Dad and Mom even bought some new, albeit cheap, imitation leather furniture for the living room, and Ann and Mom framed some artwork out of magazines - flowers of all colors. Mom seemed happy with the effort, but told Ann, "It's still a mess, it's still not very good." There was no pleasing her for Ann.

The evening Mom went to the hospital she said to Ann from the car window, "You need to pray, Ann. The baby hasn't moved for hours." She entrusted this request to her prayerful daughter alone, acknowledging that Ann had the gift of Jesus' grace. Ann moved in close to give Mom a kiss goodbye on her cheek, and Mom rolled up the car window and grimaced in pain before she could land the kiss. Ann's last remembrance of Mom was that window going up.

Ann had agreed to miss the dance at Okawville High School that night to stay home with Betty and the three little boys. She hit her knees once she had them all in bed. In Mom and Dad's bedroom, she held on tight to the little walnut cradle that had been brought down from the attic for the newborn's arrival. She prayed with all her might, to Jesus, to God, to bless them and keep them safe. When she finished her prayers, she felt a great peace. She knew that Jesus was there with them and that everything would be okay. God would answer her prayers and it would be okay. She slept soundly.

At four a.m. Ann heard Dad's footsteps on the stairs. He knew Ann would be awake. She trusted everything was all right, as she had prayed. Her single bed was right by the door and she heard him trudging up the stairs - slowly. She could tell something was wrong. The footsteps stopped on the landing as Dad cracked the door to the bedroom. Dad leaned down close, right by her face and she heard his voice quivering as he said, "We lost her. We've lost them both."

She looked intently at Dad's face. He'd aged 10 years, his face so gray and lifeless. He was crying hard as he said those words to his daughter. He slowly trudged back downstairs.

In that moment, Ann felt a cold wind come over her heart. She was shocked. She had experienced the presence of God in her prayers for them the night before, and His answer was not what she had been expecting. She felt numb. No, this can't be.

Oh, God! It was all her fault. "I didn't pray hard enough, right enough. My motivations weren't right, not pure enough. I killed them." She didn't cry and didn't move. She was so angry, angry at Jesus. In those hours of the morning Mom died, Ann shut the door to her heart to the love and comfort of Jesus. "I KILLED THEM. I always trusted you, how could you, Jesus?" Ann's heart closed to Jesus and she walked away from Him. In His place, an overwhelming guilt resided. "It was all my fault. I didn't even pray right, the one thing she asked only me to do. I've failed her again." But no tears came.

Ann wept as she told me this, 47 years later.

She didn't shed one tear in all the days of the funeral. She knows she didn't cry at all, even after the funeral when she walked out to the pasture, to one of her favorite spots. She just felt the guilt that she bore all alone, sharing it with no one. She thought we all knew Mom's request of her, but we didn't. We had no idea that she was tormented by blaming herself. I had no idea until we talked for this book.

There is a saying that "When God closes a door, he opens a window." For Ann, when her heart closed to Jesus, the one let in was the devil. Within two weeks, the "old" Ann was gone. She had so much unresolved grief, never crying, never letting it out. "I was so wounded, feeling like I'd killed Mom and our baby brother," she sobbed, as she recalled. "There were times when Mom was so hard on me, I daydreamed about life without her." Although it's quite normal for teens to have these feelings toward parents, it haunts Ann to this day.

This new Ann was filled with guilt and searching for a way to escape this wrenching, unbearable pain. Within two weeks, she found drugs, alcohol - anything to stop the pain, even for a little while. She fell in with a different crowd at Okawville High School, the "druggies." Her grades plummeted, from straight A's to just passing. She smoked weed and drank alcohol every chance she got. She just knew that when she had the money, getting high or drunk on the weekends helped ease her pain for a while.

Ann doesn't remember much of the funeral or the weeks after that. She just remembers the burning guilt. She remembers Dad picking up the baby, asking us if we wanted to hold him and Ann saying, "No, no way."

Ann remembers people coming by during the visitation, cruelly commenting, "The baby is in with her. Why would they do that?"

She remembers Dad making us all go to church the day after the funeral, to Sunday Mass and the pain in her heart as she realized Jesus was gone. All the church- goers pointing and staring at us, but not talking to us or offering comfort. She remembers Dad cooking chicken for Sunday dinner, even after Mom was gone, trying hard to keep things normal for us in the face of total abnormality.

She remembers sitting on Grandma's back porch on the day Mom died, trying to understand why we'd lost Mom. Dad's sisters were sitting inside. Aunt Veronica was crying, saying over and over, "So very sad."

Ann overheard the aunts discussing our fate, saying, "I'll take Betty or Ellen, or the boys, but not Ann." That hurt. Fortunately, Dad was wiser than to split us up. He didn't let anyone take any of us.

After Mom died, Ann was supposed to be in charge of making breakfast. She'd put the bacon on to fry in one of the big skillets and set the oatmeal to cook in another. Then, she'd go upstairs and get dressed as fast as she could. Unfortunately, it usually wasn't fast enough, because she'd come downstairs to a blackened pot, completely burnt bacon. We'd eat it anyway.

Ann would try to hide the evidence, sometimes burying the pot in the field on the east side of the house. Dad would come home tired from working and find the pot and scrub it clean. She regrets making him do that now. She seemed mad at the world and intolerant of all of us. But now she takes our teasing her, our "black pot Annie," with a smile.

Shortly after Ann turned 18, she decided it was time to leave. She packed up her few possessions and didn't even say goodbye to Dad – just left and went on with her life.

Ann moved to Centralia. She went to work at the local country club as a waitress. Ann started using harder drugs, and her language and demeanor became rough. It seemed like she was purposefully distancing herself from the rest of us – and she admits now that that was exactly what she was doing. She moved far away from the guilt and pain that we all represented. By now the reason for her behavior was deeply buried.

Ann believes her life was saved because she was afraid of needles. She didn't do the drugs that would involve shooting up.

A group of Ann's high school friends were worried about her sudden change and talked her into going with them to Carbondale to visit a counselor. Ann doesn't remember it changing anything but remembers their concern and kindness. So many of her friends from those years were overtaken by the lifestyle, dying young from drug-related overdoses, suicides or accidents. Thank God there weren't the drugs that are on the streets today, like meth and opioids, or Ann would certainly have died.

Physical affection was another way to take her mind off of her pain, and Ann was finding "love" in all the wrong places. Along Ann's journey we lost the family's first grandchild. It was to be Ann's only baby girl. She was born in the spring of 1974. Ann had gotten pregnant soon after moving out of the house. Dad drove to her apartment in Centralia when he found out and begged her, cried with her not to give the baby up for adoption.

But Ann's mind was set. She knew she couldn't give the baby a home or the mothering that this little one deserved. Neither could Dad – he was struggling with us at home. She made arrangements to have the baby adopted.

The baby's APGAR scores were good at her birth, so she believes the baby was unaffected by her lifestyle. The day the family got their little girl broke

Ann's heart. Ann has been waiting for her little girl to find her, hopeful that one day she will.

After giving up the baby, Ann went further down a path of self-destruction. She was living with even more guilt. Ann began living the "hippie" lifestyle in a home with no water or power, way out in the country. She wasn't Ann anymore - it was Annie now.

Betty and I went to visit her there just once. She made sure none of her drug friends were there that day. Annie prepared a wonderful lunch, with Mom's homemade bread on the sandwiches and a cake every bit as good as Mom's. We walked way out past a field and Annie showed us her crop – beautiful big marijuana plants, taller than we were. I remember being scared – what if someone caught us there? Then, realizing Annie was there every day, I prayed, "Oh, God, protect her."

Annie got a job as an aide at Murray Center in Centralia, Illinois, soon after moving to Centralia. It is a home for developmentally disabled children run by the State of Illinois. It is still there today, providing care for those that need it most. Due to the grace of her supervisor, Annie didn't lose her job when she turned up pregnant. The supervisor loved her own adopted grandchild more than anything on earth, and when Annie told her she was giving the baby up for adoption, acknowledged how happy that would make some family that desperately wanted a baby. She protected Annie from being fired.

When Annie was having a good day, she was great with the kids at Murray Center - kind and loving to those that needed it so badly. On most days, Annie was still functioning on the job. As her drug use intensified in the years after the baby, Annie had really bad days where she could not perform. It all finally came to a head. Her supervisor gave her a three-day suspension and told her that if she didn't straighten up her act and come back clean, she would be fired.

Annie went home, not sure what to do. She was 22, she thinks. She called one of her friends, Judy, an antique dealer that had taken Annie under her wing. Annie told her about having been suspended from her job and her supervisor's ultimatum. Annie told Judy, "I want someone to know, to get my body so it doesn't rot here as I probably won't make it. Come back in three days and check on me, please."

Annie had decided it was time – she was going to go clean. She knew how hard this was to do cold turkey and didn't know if she could do it, but she was going to try, or die. Judy, who had never talked about God in all the time Annie knew her, left her with a pamphlet that said, "God is real and will protect." Ann held onto that pamphlet all weekend.

Annie found her way back to God because of a flower. She went for a walk behind her house in the country that first day of trying to be sober and came across a beautiful flower, a daisy of some kind. Red with yellow on the inside, so intricate, Annie knew it was too beautiful to have been made by anyone in this world, so she challenged God (always the fierce one, our Annie). "If you are real, if you are God, I will be able to go to sleep tonight without drugs and wake up in the morning and not need them again. I will be in my right mind. You will protect me." She remembered, "I wanted to make changes in my life, and I wanted His help – finally! I'd never quit loving God; it was just that I was such a failure in my prayer for Mom that I couldn't serve Him. God had never moved – I did."

Annie didn't suffer withdrawals like she certainly should have. Her mind was clear when she woke up the next day - she was in her right mind. The miracle she'd asked him for! She felt good for the first time in many years.

It's not that she didn't struggle along the path of her renewed faith and sobriety, but she had turned a clear corner in her journey.

She sought some counseling for help with her grief and went to a doctor for help with continuing sobriety. She also continued to learn about scripture and was finally able to forgive herself for not praying "correctly" at Mom's death. She was able to realize it was not her fault. Annie felt healed as God set her free from the pain she had carried for those many years.

Ann was desperate for change – she finally opened the door of her heart to Jesus, and He walked back in. Ann learned that He gave her free will – to reject or accept Him – He had never gone away.

A part of her change was attributable to Lorraine Weber. The same person that had cajoled our brother Bill into going to the TEC retreat was now back in Annie's life too. Annie attended a retreat with Lorraine and felt the love of Jesus burn even more intensely in her heart. Lorraine helped Annie to gain the social skills she desperately needed, along with some other strong female mentors that helped her to heal. I hope Lorraine's family knows what a blessing she was to us.

Years later, one of Annie's co-workers at Murray Center shared this thought with her: "I knew there had to be a God when I saw your transformation," referring to her conversion and the change that came upon her when she let God back into her life. Annie's language and demeanor changed back to that gracious person she was before.

Annie is grateful, for God has forgiven and given her so much.

Annie has studied and knows the scripture well now and the passage she recalled for me as we talked was, "Satan comes to kill, steal and destroy." He almost won with Annie; we are blessed that he didn't. Her emotional healing from Mom's abuse will take much longer. Annie describes that as "a work in progress."

As Annie worked her way through her newfound Christianity, she went back to college and did well at Murray Center. "I wanted to fulfill Mom's wish for all of us to do better than they did in life, to have a profession. I wanted to do something right, something she'd be proud of," Annie said.

She also found Jim and they fell in love. They met at a Christian church function and married a few months later, when she was 28. Jim knows all about Annie's past and loves her just for who she is - an acceptance for which she'd searched all of her life. Their love for each other and strong faith made all the difference in Annie's life, bringing her true happiness.

Jim was so kind to Annie; he helped her to heal and made her feel valued. Once when Dad was giving Annie grief about something he thought she'd done wrong and swore at her, Jim rose up from his chair to his full six-foot-three-inch height and put a finger on Dad's chest saying, "That is my wife, you will not talk to her like that again." Annie loved her husband for defending her and making her realize she had worth, value. Dad never spoke to Annie like that again.

Jim saw Annie as the wonderful woman she was, as God saw her, and cajoled her into accepting the role of parent – to not fear being a mother. When she had their first son, Josiah, he patiently guided her to not parent in her mother's fashion and to love her child just for who he was.

When Annie was pregnant with their second son, Noah, she was finally given the peace for which she'd prayed all those years. She was cleaning the bathroom at their home in Mt. Vernon. She had been thinking of Mom. The flood gates opened and Annie cried, finally, and told Mom how sorry she was - sorry she'd not prayed well enough the night she and the baby had died. Telling her how much she would have loved her grandchildren; that they were not like Annie. Annie had buried her grief for so long - it had taken Annie all those years to cry for Mom and let that grief out. She finally felt a level of peace with Mom's death.

Annie's guilt for not having prayed correctly and killing Mom and Robert wasn't rational or Biblical, but it was very real to her 15-year-old soul. As the years passed, Ann's wounds from that guilt scabbed over, not healing, just always there. She didn't always think of Mom and her guilt; she just knew she was in pain. As Annie and I talked about our past, she described it like this: "We all went on with our lives – we moved on. We still hurt so bad, but we didn't acknowledge the pain we were in was from our grief. Our lives just went on, as they had to."

What's troubling is that no one other than her concerned friends - not Dad nor an aunt nor a teacher nor me for that matter - tried to intervene. No one sat her down and asked, "What are you doing? Why have you changed so drastically?" No one knew Annie's deep despair, her guilt for failing to pray adequately, her conviction that she was responsible for their deaths. No one asked her, "Why?"

Annie, in her normal intense fashion, threw herself into her newfound Christianity. She quit her job at Murray Center after Noah was born and became active in their Christian Church. She and Jim served their church as missionary coordinators for many years, taking numerous mission trips to five continents and 17 countries. They preached His word on marriage and family to so many people.

Annie is also the one closest to following Mom's true calling. Annie is an excellent homesteader. She raises chickens, guinea hens and bunnies on their small farm. She is so good at it, just like Mom was good at making the ramshackle farm into a productive homestead. Annie's vegetable garden is as large and bountiful each year as Mom's had been. Annie is the one who carries on the canning of the produce and the quest for organic everything. She is the expert bread baker, slapping it on the table just like Mom did, with the same intention.

Annie remembers Gary giving us gifts that first Christmas without Mom. Gary baled hay and trapped and sold furs - he worked so hard all the time. He gave each girl perfume - Chantilly Lace. And the boys got toys. Gary sloughed this off, like it was no big deal, but his kindness was a big deal to Annie.

Annie doesn't remember Dad's nervous breakdown like I do. She remembers the ambulance coming and the drivers saying to Dad, "You need to straighten up, you've got these kids here to take care of." Dad going to bed, but staying home that night. She does remember the social services person and thinking, "Oh crap." She remembers asking Dad if they were going to take us away and Dad saying, "Don't worry about it" and it all turning out okay as Social Services didn't come back.

Annie teaches homesteading at a local farm store and has also taught at the local community colleges. She writes a blog on homesteading, where she shares her wealth of knowledge on all things homesteading. I can just see Mom beaming down on her accomplishments.

Annie still hears, "I wish you were more like your sister, Ellen," when she thinks of Mom. I told Annie as we talked for this book, that I had spent my youth trying to be more like her. Ann always seemed to be the center of everyone's attention, doing exciting, creative things, and I wanted so much to be more like that. Ann got everything new, and I got her hand-me-downs and was jealous. I just wanted to be Ann. Annie thought I learned from what she did wrong, what angered Mom and I learned what not to do. From my viewpoint, Ann was stating her mind; I was holding my tongue. It took me years to learn to express my opinion.

I thank God for and cherish the blessing of the close friendship Annie and I now have.

Annie learned through her dark years that positives can come out of the negatives. When on the mission field, no youth could pull one over on her – she'd seen it all. She'd tell them her story of the years she struggled without Jesus in her life and knows it was impactful to some of them. They would come and open up to her. She'd listen, knowing the big solution ahead for them was Jesus.

She had an "AHA!" moment on the mission field when she was particularly hard on a young girl. Annie saw real potential in this girl, but the girl was not fulfilling it at all. Annie was relentless, challenging her to do better, giving her the hardest chores. She realized, "That's what Mom saw in me – what Mom wanted for me – to have my potential fulfilled. Sadly, Mom didn't know the parenting techniques to produce what she wanted in me."

Annie will find out one day when she meets Mom in heaven if she got that right. I think through it all, she did. Ann doesn't expect she will have Mom's favor, even in heaven. "We won't have little houses next to each other in heaven, me and Mom. I'll be closer to Dad," Annie smiled and said.

I treasure knowing the reason for Annie's past now and regret that I didn't try to intervene back then. Ann has spent a lifetime trying to do something right that would make Mom proud. Annie honors her mother for giving her life. She will always be her daughter. She will never know how it would have been different if Mom had lived.

Annie learned that God is a God of second chances. "I can't change the consequences of my past, but have learned that God is always there to forgive me. God's mercies are new every morning."

"I'm praying that telling the story of my painful past will help others that are struggling to go and get help with their grief - to not travel down the destructive paths that I did," Annie says hopefully.

I hope Annie has lots of days ahead filled with His peace as the sun rises on Grandma Mueller's back porch. That's one reason Jim agreed to move to her family's home-place, because Annie feels Jesus' presence, peace and love on that porch.

Chapter 15

Gary

Work, work, work
All day long
That became
Gary's song

When she sees him
Mom will say with delight
"You kept them together,
Everything was all right"

Photographs in the 1950s were not the easy, digital process they are today, where we have thousands of them at our fingertips on our phones. They were expensive and done only on special occasions. In the Mueller family photo archive, there are hundreds of snapshots and a few professional photographs. In those precious photographic memories of infants and toddlers, eighty percent of them are of the firstborn, Gary. Maybe ten percent were of Ann, about five percent were of me and the remaining four siblings - well, there just aren't many. There are all possible angles and shots of Gary.

Gary Fred was the first, born after Mom and Dad had been married a few years. They were so ready for the blessing of their firstborn, this adorable little blond-haired, blue-eyed child.

As the oldest, Gary always held a special spot in the family. He earned that spot. He was Dad's right hand on the farm. Especially since the next three children were girls, Gary shouldered a lot of the chores. He was the one Mom relied on to cut the grass and lift heavy things when Dad was gone. He was the biggest and could easily have been like some of my friends' big brothers that were mean. But that wasn't his nature, and he didn't need to be that way. We six younger kids looked up to our big brother while we were growing up.

So I was worried when we sat down to discuss this book. My big brother Gary was fiddling with his shirt tail, rolling it over and over between his fingers. His eyes brimmed up with tears as soon as we got started talking. It had been 47 years, and he and I had never spoken of Mom's death, or how we felt about it, or how we'd handled our grief. I could tell he was nervous to do so now. I would soon know why.

Mom had a system for communicating with Dad and Gary when they were out working in the field. Now it's easy, just call on a cell phone, but back in those days, it was a problem. Mom devised a system that allowed them to communicate even when they were in the field and far from the house. Dad raised a flag pole on the south side of the pole-barn. It was the highest spot on the farmstead. There were three flags that could be raised. The white flag, which meant all was fine, flew most of the time. A green flag meant come home, but no rush - like lunch is ready to eat. The red flag meant get back home right now as quickly as you can: it's an emergency.

The Friday evening of September 25, 1970, the night Mom died, Gary was harvesting beans in the south field about three eighths of a mile from the house. He had gotten on the combine right after school was out so that he could get a good start before dark. It was habit to look over at the flag from time to time, and when Gary saw the red flag had been raised, he knew to get back quickly. He hurried into the house. Mom had her bag packed and in the 1960 Chevy station wagon. "I need to go now, Gary. You'll need to drive me," Mom said. "The baby is coming." Gary was panicked, not wanting to have to be the one to take her; it was Dad's place, not his. Not his responsibility – he was only 16, turning 17 the next month. Dad wasn't home from work yet, so there wasn't a choice.

Gary went to quickly clean up. I was to go to the Freshman Orientation, and Ann volunteered to stay with the little boys and Betty. Gary and Mom were just pulling out of the driveway when Dad pulled up, thank God. Even though Mom and Dad fought sometimes, they were a good team, and she needed him by her side that night. Dad said, "I'll take it from here, son." Gary remembers feeling so relieved. We seven kids all gathered around them and waved goodbye as they sped off to the hospital.

Gary went to the high school that evening, and after the Freshman Orientation was over, there was a dance for the upperclassmen. He had a good time dancing with his classmates. Gary wasn't one of those popular kids like the basketball jocks or the "bad boys." He was smart as a tack and a genuinely nice, down-to-earth farm boy.

Gary and Mom had a plan for his future. He had just started his senior year of high school. He had made excellent grades, was near the top of his class and was all set to get an Illinois State Scholarship. Mom had helped him apply for it and it would take care of all the tuition costs for his bachelor's degree. They'd only have to come up with money for expenses. He'd go to Belleville Area College for two years and live at home. That way he could still help with the farm and get a side job when he wasn't in class. Then, he'd go on to Rolla for an engineering degree.

He'd be the first of us Mueller children to graduate from college, the first Schmersahl grandchild to go to college. This was their plan and Gary was excited for his future, hopeful that it would all work. Dad wasn't so sold on Gary going to college, but Mom was convincing; she insisted that he must get an education. We all rooted for him, because he would set the pace for the rest of us to go.

Gary didn't get home from the dance until almost midnight that fateful night. Dad wasn't back yet. Gary went straight to bed knowing he'd have a hard day in the field harvesting the rest of the beans tomorrow and excited about the news of the new arrival that would await him in the morning.

The alarm usually blared the "Our Father" on KMOX radio at six a.m. sharp, but it didn't that morning. Gary didn't wake up until around seven. He stumbled down the stairs and on the last step sat Ann and me, crying. He took one look at us and knew something was horribly wrong. Ann blurted out, "Mom's dead, so is baby."

Gary felt a sledgehammer hitting him up the side of the head. He nearly blacked out. "Can't be, what did she say?"

Dad came into the living room then, took Gary by the arm and said, "Let's take a walk, son." During that walk, Gary lost his youth and his hope of being an engineer. His childhood days of dances and dreams ended.

Dad held on to Gary's arm, and they walked past the machine shed down past the pond east of the house to the big cottonwood tree by the creek. The site of so many picnics where the family would throw down a big quilt and Mom would serve up tasty fried chicken or sandwiches on homemade bread. We'd eat with our fingers while we'd savor the sunshine. There was no sunshine this morning.

Dad said to Gary, "I need your help. I can't do this by myself. I need you to grow up, step up, stay here and help me raise these kids. Stay here on the farm and help me." Gary felt that sledgehammer again – Wham! His plan was gone. His dream of college gone. Mom gone.

Dad had done as much for his mother after his own dad had died, staying home and helping her raise his five sisters. He had not married until he was almost 30 and then found someone that was happy to live across the field from his mother. I think Dad may have expected the same loyalty and help from his oldest son, Gary.

Soon, Dad was gone too. He went into the bottle - deep. Gary would be the one to get the call from the tavern when he was too drunk to drive home: "Come and get your dad; we can't let him drive like this."

It was Gary that Dad leaned on for the farm chores and to be sure things got done – feeding the animals, planting the crops, you name it. Not that Dad didn't work too, because he did – it's just that Gary became the responsible adult in the home as Dad sank, unable to cope with his grief.

On that walk that morning just after Mom died, Dad strategized with Gary about how to pay for the funeral, as Mom didn't have life insurance. Such a hard conversation to have with a teenager that had just lost his Mom. Gary knew that Dad needed him, so he stepped up. He was the one who really made the decisions that day when we went to Moll Funeral Home as Dad stared blankly, just unable to function. Gary was there helping him, picking out the coffin and figuring out who would be the pallbearers. By the end of the day, it was arranged.

Gary has few memories of the funeral and the next few days. He remembers how touched he felt, surprised that so many of his high school classmates came to the funeral home that evening. He remembers walking in to the funeral Mass and seeing that the church was packed full. Everyone in St. Libory must have been there. He remembers the parish priest stumbling up the altar as he processed in at the beginning of the Mass, and not making much sense during his sermon.

After her services were over, Dad drove us all home in our Chevy station wagon. Dad went straight to bed, exhausted. Gary looked around at the yard that Mom loved and saw the need to get it cleaned up one last time for the year. He got out the push mower and cut the grass, making it look just like she would have liked.

And he kept working. Work was the way Gary coped with his grief. "Don't think about missing her, or this pain in my heart, just focus on the work; on what has to get done. Work will keep my mind off of it," Gary shared. And work Gary did. Not just at our farm. He worked for the local tractor dealership, for the township road commissioner and at an auto body shop. He still works harder than anyone I know.

Gary's few close friends were of comfort to him. "But none of that crying around stuff, they were just there for me," he stated.

He did receive the Illinois State Scholarship that paid his tuition, and he enrolled at Belleville Area College in 1971. He attended classes for a couple of semesters and then quit school. He could see he wasn't going to be able to go on to Rolla, as there was no way he could leave the boys alone with Dad, not in the state Dad was in much of the time.

He didn't leave. Gary went to work full-time after he dropped out, and then got married at 21. He lived nearby and came home often to help Dad on the farm and to be sure the boys were okay. Gary was the one that made sure they stayed together, as we girls were all out of the house by age 18, as Dad had insisted.

Gary was almost forced to leave home and fight in the Vietnam War. He had a high draft number in 1975 and had received orders to report to San Diego in June. When Saigon fell in April 1975 he recalls the news commentator stating, "Anyone with deployment papers call your draft board to verify that you do not have to go." He called and he didn't have to go, but regrets not serving. He'd have been assured of not being deployed since the war was over, and all of the branches of the military wanted him to join. Dad didn't want him to go, so he didn't.

Mom's death impacted Gary perhaps more than any of us. As the oldest, he bore the brunt of dealing with Dad. Dad listened to Gary more than any of the rest of us. Even though Dad didn't really hear anything but the bottle during those dark years.

Gary doesn't remember Dad's nervous breakdown in the months after Mom's death as I do. Another event that he does recall vividly caused a rift between father and son. It was several years after Mom had died. Dad had been drinking. Gary and the boys were baling hay for the cattle we had again that year. It was early afternoon; Dad came home and drove out to the field, loudly spouting off about his ability to work too. He fell off the hay wagon, passing out. Gary picked him up and took him to the Sparta Hospital, where they kept him for a few days while his injuries from the fall healed and for observation.

When Dad got back home, he threatened Gary, "Don't you ever do that again," and Gary felt Dad secretly hated him after that incident. That feeling hurt as badly as losing Mom, after all he had sacrificed.

Gary believes that Dad's marriage to Ardell was divine intervention. She was a saint when it came to "the old man", i.e., Dad. Gary would do anything for Ardell: she saved Dad from self-destruction. Without Ardell, Gary is sure Dad would have been gone soon, that he would have run into something or, worse yet, killed someone while driving drunk.

Gary may not be a strong Bible beater or a church-going Catholic, but he believes in God and that there is an afterlife. That at the end of each of our lives there will be a clear accounting for how we've lived. Gary envisions it like this: for every bad thing we've done, there's a scoop of cockleburs put into our bushel basket, and for every good thing we've done a scoop of corn is put into another basket. The goal is to have a lot more weight in the corn basket. "The thing to remember is that corn is a lot heavier than cockleburs, thank goodness," Gary laughed and continued, "The kindnesses we pay to those that need it most, such as giving to the poorest among us, will be rewarded." Gary has always been good at that kind of deep, thoughtful analogy.

Gary expresses his emotions not through talking, but through writing. He's penned the most beautiful sentiments over the years in cards that I'll always treasure. He's also pretty expressive with the expletives, which I've taken out of this "G-Rated" book. That rough exterior hides the softie that cares deeply for all of his siblings, and always has.

Gary can't remember Mom – the sledgehammer to his head that morning of her death knocked her out of his memory. When he visits her grave, he sees the picture on the tombstone of her in that pretty green dress from Aunt Eleanor's wedding, and he knows it's her. There's not much else. He does remember the things she cooked and baked. He's the one with the turtle mulligan recipe.

We had a couple of ponds on the farm, and we'd swim there on hot summer days. Gary remembers Mom yelling at him, "Gary, you watch those girls." He was always responsible for us. Dad and Gary would catch turtles in the ponds, and we'd make mulligan in a huge black kettle. Gary has replicated that mulligan – it's delicious! As is his custard pie with a crust as flaky as Mom's and the custard filling baked to perfection. He worked for years to get it just right, and we all beg him to bring it to family holiday parties.

He doesn't get to eat much of it, though. Gary is the one of the siblings that is afflicted with the family curse that took our grandparents so early in their lives: diabetes. He is an insulin-dependent type two diabetic, diagnosed two decades ago and struggling to keep his blood sugar levels under control.

Gary was nervous to talk with me about Mom's death and the impact it had on his life. Tears spilled from my big brother's eyes as he remembered Dad's plea for his help on their walk that morning. He'd never shared that experience with anyone. Tears spilled again when he voiced how different he thinks his life would have been if Mom had lived. He would not have had to grow up in that moment and accept so much responsibility. He'd have graduated from college and gone on to design and build all sorts of things. We'll never know.

Gary summed it up for me this way: "You can write about it all you want, Ellen, and discuss and re-discuss the issues. In every tragic moment, for every horrible detail dealt you in life, there is never healing to a whole. There is never full resolution - there is only reconciliation - no, more, no less. That's all humans are capable of. We will only fully know the answer to 'Why?' when it's time. And if we can read this, it ain't time yet."

When his day of accounting is here, I believe Mom will be there with the biggest hug and thank you to her firstborn, who gave up his dream and helped us all stay together, who grew up that day she died.

Chapter 16

Dad's Gone

Our Dad was a man of dichotomies
Proud, yet humble as a man could be

He taught us to work and to tell the truth
He loved the land, and to fish, hunt and shoot

Stoic and German, like men in that era
And most of us see him when we look in the mirror

And, as time passed, we understood
Our Dad, he did the best he could

We hope that he's with Mom, up in heaven
Watching over us, their flock of seven

As I was researching family photos for this book, I came across some old postcards from 1947, several years before Mom and Dad were married. They were sent by Dad to his Mother, Mary, from scenic places out west in Colorado and Utah. "Saw some wonderful things in Yellowstone Park yesterday. Everything's O.K." he wrote her.

I never knew my Dad had traveled anywhere, except that one trip to Kentucky he and Mom took after Gary was born. I was shocked. I thought I knew all of our family's stories. My siblings didn't know about this trip either. Made me wonder what else we didn't know about Dad.

What I did know about Dad seemed to be full of contradictions. He would be furious when we didn't date Catholics, but he married Ardell who was not one. He would sell portions of our small farm to make ends meet, then use the proceeds to buy timber ground for hunting which produced no income. He was generous with his time with his hunting and tavern buddies, but didn't make time to be there for his children after we lost Mom.

We've already talked about his drinking and what affect that had on us, so I won't belabor that part of Dad. He, even when drinking, was a very kind person. Kind, like he'd go out of his way to help others, especially if they were an underdog, even if he didn't know them well. Like taking Julie, the housekeeper, into our home near the end of her life.

And honest. That's probably why he was the Union Steward for the Carpenter's Local on most of his jobs. He could be trusted to do the right thing. He expected as much from his children too. If you really wanted to hurt Dad, lying to him worked. I am sorry to say I learned that lesson several times, the hard way, by lying to him and getting caught. I did eventually learn the "truthful is best" lesson. I think we all did.

And stubborn. Once Dad made up his mind on something, only Mom, and later Ardell, could sway him. Many of the seven of us have that stubborn trait too.

And Dad was hardworking. He and Mom both provided the example of working hard to their children; an example that has served us all well. That work ethic gave us the ability to accomplish many things in each of our lives, in spite of obstacles.

The song "You've Got to Stand for Something" always makes me think of our Dad. He stood up for what he thought was right. The chorus of that song says, "You've got to stand for something, or you'll fall for anything, you've got to be your own man, not a puppet on a string. Never compromise what's right, and uphold your family name...." Those words are Dad.

Before Mom's death, Dad had a twinkle in his eyes, a good sense of humor and loved to tease and joke around. During those seven years after Mom's death and before he married Ardell, the years most of this book describes, Dad was different. He had a quiet desperation, a profound sadness about him most of the time.

His demeanor changed dramatically after he married Ardell, however. More like the Dad I knew growing up that enjoyed life. His twinkle was back! Ardell reigned in his drinking and occasional erratic behavior. During their 20 years together, Dad seemed happy.

Married the same number of years to Delores and to Ardell, I sometimes wonder which of Tony Mueller's loves had made him happier.

In all the time I knew Dad, he seemed happiest after he retired, and he and Ardell moved back to her house in Waterloo, Illinois in 1987. Waterloo was a small town about an hour from St. Libory. I suspect Dad was happy because he finally didn't have all that hard work as a carpenter and on the farm. He didn't have the responsibility of caring for his Mother. Retired at last. He seemed at peace.

A small yard to mow, and the grandkids of a dozen children to come visit Grandpa Tony. He fished often and walked up to the corner tavern occasionally, where he made a whole new group of friends. He and Ardell didn't have a lot, just enough income from their Social Security and his carpenter's pension to enjoy their last years.

The retirement bliss didn't last long.

Dad started losing weight and just feeling sluggish and tired early in 1992. He was diagnosed with Chronic Lymphocytic Leukemia (CLL), a type of cancer of the blood and bone marrow. We were all in shock. There wasn't cancer in our family. Diabetes, sure, but not cancer. Stroke, yes, but not cancer. His prognosis was so uncertain. All the research the seven of us could do didn't give us many clear answers - the disease may progress quickly or it may lay dormant and not affect him for years.

Unfortunately, Dad's CLL was aggressive. He was given very strong chemotherapy drugs, which had horrific side effects. He continued losing weight. His stomach was constantly churning and nothing tasted good to him. Alcohol was now forbidden. Sober, not by his choice, but by necessity. This was the start of his long, five-year battle with his cancer.

Bill and I had moved several times as my career progressed with Illinois Power. Dad had only been to our home in Decatur once, when Annie had brought Dad and Ardell up to Decatur as a wonderful surprise for us. Annie was thoughtful like that. Dad didn't drive much out of the local area, so I understood why he hadn't come more often. Dad hadn't even been to our newest location in Bethalto. So, when our son, Ab, made his first communion that spring in 1992, I called and offered to come pick him up so he and Ardell could be with the family for this important celebration.

I'd been proud of us for raising our children Catholic, just as Bill promised Dad he would when it was a condition Dad imposed before he gave his blessing for our marriage. Years later, after the kids were in college, we decided to join Bill's home church, St. Peters United Church of Christ in Okawville. Bill had spent 25 years attending my church: it was my turn to go to his. We both feel so at home there now.

On my phone call to her, Ardell flatly said of the invitation to Ab's big day, "We won't be coming, Ellen." No explanation other than that.

I was so hurt. I started crying after the phone call, and my daughter Joy, who was 11 at the time, very sweetly consoled me, "It will be all right, Mom."

About an hour later, Ardell called me and asked, "Did you know Joy called your father?"

"No, I didn't, what did she say?"

"She told him he needed to come to Ab's first communion. It was important to my Mom, and that he was not a nice person because he made my Mom cry."

This was one of those situations parents often face when you are pleased and displeased with a child at the same time. I was proud of Joy for standing up for me, for trying to make things the way I needed them to be. I was not proud of her for talking to her Grandpa in a disrespectful way. We had a, "You did such a nice thing in a not nice way," discussion. In my heart, I will always love that she tried.

During that phone call, Ardell told me that they couldn't come because of Dad's health. The chemo treatments he'd started a month earlier made him just too weak right now. If she'd said so earlier, I'd have certainly understood. I had no idea he was in such a weakened condition already. He always said he was "just fine" when we asked him how he was on the phone. She said Dad had asked her not to tell me, as he didn't want us kids to know and to worry or feel sorry for him. Stoic even in the face of cancer. That was classic Dad.

What I'd totally forgotten was the letter Dad wrote to me after that incident. I've struggled with my relationship with my Dad my whole life, wanting him so badly to say those words, "I love you" and never hearing them. Maybe I wasn't listening well enough.

After his mother's death in 1985, Dad held an auction to sell our family home and contents and the last 20 acres of farm ground in 1987. My husband Bill bought me my Mom's cedar chest, which was where we stored all of our family's precious memorabilia: cards, letters, pictures, children's artwork, etc. When we moved last year, it was somehow turned upside down and the treasures became all jumbled up. I kept being drawn to the chest, like it was calling me to get it organized.

It took me an evening to straighten out; it was such a mess! One of the last pieces of paper I sorted through took my breath away: a letter from my Dad that I didn't remember at all.

This is the letter, the only letter I have that he ever wrote me:

Ellen:
Please forgive me for hurting your feelings when you called. I guess Joy told you what I told her, but there is a lot I would like to talk to you about.
I will call you or you can call me and I will tell you why. Ardell & I are both sad that I can not be with Ab. and his family on such an important day in a young man's life.
We both love you and your family very much, but there are some things that I can not do anymore. I hope you understand

He really did say he loved me! I just didn't acknowledge it then or remember the letter. So self-absorbed with all the things I had going on with my career and my own family, I never went to see him and talk with him as he asked me to. Just called and talked with Ardell briefly.

With the help of the Koinonia retreats and growing older (obviously not wiser, but at least more reflective), I have realized now, so many years later, that he did love me. I told Dad I loved him on his deathbed. He didn't say it back like I thought he would. That hurt, but I'm glad at least to have told him. Yet, I'd not really forgiven him in my heart, as Jesus asks us to, for those painful seven years after we lost Mom. Or asked Dad and His forgiveness for those years I was hate-filled and not as helpful as I should have been. Maybe that was another purpose for me in writing this book, to enable me to finally come to peace with my Dad?

My brother Bill and I talked about our feelings for Dad as he grew sicker from the leukemia in the summer of 1997. I encouraged Bill to go talk to Dad and tell him how he felt, even if the words were not returned. It would eat Bill up to have that regret the rest of his life if he didn't.

Bill went to the hospital when Ardell called to say Dad's time was near, determined to tell him he loved him (which you will remember, dear reader, are very hard words for my brother Bill to say), to let him know he'd forgiven him in his heart. As soon as he arrived Dad asked Bill to help him with some legal issues. Dad had never asked Bill for legal help. Dad hated lawyers and had derided and made jokes about Bill's profession every chance he had, which hurt Bill all those years.

Bill was understandably proud that Dad had, finally, maybe, accepted his career choice and expertise and needed his help. He put on his professional face and demeanor to talk like a lawyer, and they talked about Dad's legal concerns. Bill thought, "I will talk with Dad tomorrow about my forgiveness and love for him."

Bill never got the chance. Dad slipped into unconsciousness and died the next day. Maybe God knew Dad's need to acknowledge his son's career was stronger than Bill's need to voice his forgiveness?

Annie visited Dad often, staying close to him and Ardell. Annie and Dad had many discussions as he neared the end of his life, and he shared many stories and secrets with Ann. She took the time to sit at his bedside and listen when some of us, like me, did not.

Dad told Annie about his deep love for our Mom. How they were a good team, working together. How he respected Mom too. Respected her opinions and that she could voice them loudly, argue, and in the morning, it was over. He talked about how Mom pushed him to leave his comfortable job at the small local carpentry shop and become a union piledriver. It was Mom who wanted that for him, not Dad wanting it for himself.

He told Ann how much he loved her and each of us and what a blessing we'd been to him through all those years. Ann teased Dad and asked him, "How many of us were 'mistakes?'" and Dad indignantly replying, "You all were planned for and loved." Ann was genuinely surprised. She related that Dad was shocked that we'd ever question his love; he assumed we knew. "He tried so hard, he did the best he could," Ann says of Dad's parenting.

Dad is the one Annie misses, not Mom. She'll see someone with his haircut and smile. As she sat one afternoon with him in those last days, Dad finally shared with her the story of how Mom really died that night.

Dr. Frank P. Gaunt was our family physician. His practice was in the nearby town, Marissa. He'd seen Mom through all of her health issues and pregnancies, and he was there for her with this one too. He'd left the delivery room at St. Clement's in Red Bud that night for a brief rest, certain the baby's arrival was a little way off. It was around midnight. A young nurse, fresh out of nursing school, was left to attend Mom.

The young nurse saw the baby's head crowning, and that the baby appeared blue. She panicked. Instead of calling for the doctor, she quickly pulled the baby out of the birth canal, trying to save him. As she did so, she tore the placenta, and the amniotic fluid entered Mom's bloodstream. As no oxygen was administered to the baby, he died in the nurse's arms.

By the time Dr. Gaunt got there, Mom was struggling to survive. He worked for two hours to save her, but he couldn't. Dad was called in to say goodbye to her when Dr. Gaunt realized he wasn't going to be able to save her life. I can't imagine the feeling of helplessness Dad had as he watched his love, his wife, his partner, the mother of his children, suffer and then leave us all forever. This is how Dad sadly remembered it with Annie.

The death certificate Dr. Gaunt signed indicated that Robert Albert died at 12:24 a.m. on September 26th during labor. It stated he was not stillborn. He died from "anoxia due to mechanical strangulation, umbilical cord around neck X's 4."

Delores Ann Mueller's death certificate states that she died at 2:25 a.m. on September 26th from "pulmonary edema, acute, due to amniotic fluid embolism." Which means that the clots that formed from the amniotic fluid entered her bloodstream and went to her heart, causing fluid to fill her lungs and kill her. "Blood clots to her heart," the explanation we overheard whispered the morning she died, is close.

I can only imagine the guilt that young nurse carried with her all these years.

Dr. Gaunt performed an autopsy, but it was not recorded in the county courthouse, as the autopsy was not required by the coroner. There was no record of an autopsy or other information available at the hospital from all those years ago. Dad's account to Annie will stand as the record.

Annie also learned from Dad that the nuns at the Ruma Convent, where Mom's older sister, Sister Benigna, was serving had adopted our family as a "special project." They prayed for us all every day. This blessing was so valuable, yet we didn't even know about it. Their prayers were probably responsible for some of the saving graces we all experienced and why we were able to survive those years after we lost Mom. This may be how we managed to stay together.

Annie also recalled an attorney coming to the house just a couple of weeks or so after Mom's death. The attorney was sitting at our table in the kitchen with Dad. Ann was in the front entryway, listening. "I can get you a great settlement," the attorney said. "You can raise your kids in a life of luxury." Dad just listened, and when the attorney was finished with his pitch, Dad was quiet for a long time, tears rolling down his face.

Dad finally said, "Only if you can bring back my wife and child will I sue. Now, get out of my house!" and he proceeded to show the attorney the door. Dad may not have been able to quote scripture well, but his practice of it was a great example for his family. Vengeance was not in his vocabulary.

The attorney was probably right; we had a case for a heck of a lawsuit. Dad told Annie, "Dr. Gaunt and everyone there worked hard to save her; it would not be the right thing to sue them. Dr. Gaunt was crying as hard as I was. It would not have brought them back."

Annie suggests that what Dad really didn't have in his life was a mentor, some male figure to help guide him on how to behave, how to manage what life threw at him. If he'd have had that kind of a role model and guidance, perhaps he would have coped with Mom's traumatic death and his grief in a better manner.

Annie began an overt campaign to get Dad to be more affectionate in his final years. She started with just a sideways hug, sneaking up on him and saying "I love you, Dad." "He would stiffen up and just stand there. I kept doing it, and eventually he would hug me back and give me a kiss on the cheek," Annie smiles as she tells me. Her husband, Jim, taught Annie this technique, as he had done this with his dad. Jim's dad, like ours and many men from that era, was a "hard nut to crack" when it came to feelings. As Annie relates, when you do, you get to the sweetest meat inside.

Dad mellowed with his grandchildren too, with big hugs for them all.

Ardell called us all to let us know as Dad's time drew near. It was a Monday morning, August 18, 1997. It was time to come see him one last time, to say goodbye. He was just a shadow of himself, ghostly-looking, gaunt and gray. All of us except Tom got there to see him in the days before he passed on August 19th.

Dan is still upset because he didn't get there in time to say goodbye. Dan got the call early Tuesday morning, the 19th, that Dad wasn't doing well. Dan was working for the USDA in Casey, Illinois, which is about three hours from our home. Dan had requested a transfer to the USDA office in Greenville, Illinois earlier that year to be closer to family and the transfer and move was all set for the following month, in September.

Dan had a premonition that he'd be getting a call to come home, telling a co-worker at the end of the work day on Monday that he might not be in to work the next day. He had a feeling something was happening with Dad and he may need to drive home.

Dan left as soon as he got the call that morning and made good time until he got to the Poplar Street Bridge, which is the bridge that crosses the Mississippi River into Missouri. Dad was at Missouri Baptist Hospital, about 30 minutes west of the river. "I was so frustrated because there was an accident on the bridge, just a half mile or so in front of me. I sat on that bridge for three and a half hours, worrying, and feeling like Dad was slipping away from me – and there was nothing I could do." Dan fumed, "I didn't get to tell him goodbye, I didn't get to tell him anything."

Dan recalls matter-of-factly, "I was there, along with all of us except Tom to make the decision to stop life support. We all knew and agreed it was what Dad wanted us to do, but it was gut-wrenching nonetheless. I watched the three lines of his monitors make that familiar 'blip, blip, blip' and move up and down rhythmically. And I watched them one by one stop and a flat line appear. He was gone."

Dan remembers the six of us talking about arrangements for Dad – who the pallbearers should be, service times – in the hour after he had passed. One of Ardell's daughters-in-law was upset by this, saying to Dan, "How can you talk about this so soon. He just died!"

Dan remembers saying, "Well, we were prepared for this one: we all knew it was coming soon."

Tom was in Pensacola, Florida when he got the call from Ardell to come home quickly. Tom was exhausted, having hosted a large conference for work the three days prior, and was so looking forward to relaxing with Sara and the kids on the beach. Instead they drove straight to Illinois, trying hard to make it home and see Dad one last time. He didn't make it. Tom and family didn't arrive until right before the visitation started. Tom said, "It was okay not to see him again. I'd spent lots of good days visiting Dad during his last years, making sure my children knew him and Grandma Ardell."

Dad had remained a member of St. Libory Church, and we went back to the Moll Funeral Home, where we'd had Mom's visitation to arrange the visitation for Dad, and to the big, beautiful church in St. Libory for the funeral. He's also buried in the cemetery right by the church.

There were so many people at the visitation, and we all stood in that long row after Ardell. I was working for Illinois Power and was touched by how many of my co-workers came from across the state or sent cards or flowers. I remember each of their kind expressions of sympathy and appreciate them so much.

After the visitation, the seven of us and our families went to the little bar just down the street from the funeral home in St. Libory. We raised a toast to Dad and re-told those funny, quirky family stories with our children all seated around the table. We thought Dad would have liked that!

Dad's death and funeral were not the traumatic, disruptive event our Mom's had been 27 years prior. Betty and I discussed that we were embarrassed by how few details we could recall. We'd had time to prepare ourselves as he struggled. The loss was still very real and hard for us, but the shock was so much less. As adults, we could accept Dad's death, and we had each other and our spouses to lean on for comfort. When we lost Dad, we grieved together instead of in our own worlds, as we had at Mom's loss.

Gary was named the executor of Dad's estate, and with Bill and Kathy's help, they devised an "auction" to divide his possessions. There wasn't property left that Dad owned and Ardell rightly kept what little money they had. The Mueller family items Dad hadn't sold in their moving auction, and had moved from the farm to Ardell's house, those were ours. Nothing valuable, mind you, just our treasures.

All the items were spread on a table in Bill's basement, and each sibling drew a number. High draw went first, and we picked items until the table was cleared. The touching thing was that we were all sensitive to each other's desires, trying to not pick other's first choices and trading items when all the treasures were picked, making sure everyone was satisfied.

Gary chose Dad's 12-gauge Browning shotgun, Annie picked the family oil lamp, I selected the wooden crucifix that hung above Mom and Dad's bed, Betty chose the rocking chair that Dad always sat in, Bill selected an antique family chair, Tom picked Dad's woodworking tools and his handmade toolbox, and Dan chose Dad's 16-gauge Browning shotgun.

It was tense as the process started, but we pretty quickly ended up laughing that raucous laughter for which our family was known.

At the end of the day, the thing that tears many families apart, splitting up the inheritance, drew us even closer together.

We may not have known everything about our Dad, but we know that both Dad and Mom would have been proud of us that day!

Chapter 17

Learnings

As I talked with my siblings for this book, I learned so much. We laughed and cried. Understanding how they reacted and what they lost and missed after Mom's death was humbling. I was right there with them, but never knew their struggles. Never realized they were questioning their faith as much as I. Never understood their feelings, how they coped with their grief, or how it influenced them to be the people they are today.

They provided such diverse answers to the interview questions I used to guide the discussions for this book. The only fairly consistent answer was to Question 33, "If you could go back and say anything to her, what would it be?" Most of my siblings replied with some version of, "Don't get pregnant and leave us."

I feel truly blessed to have had the opportunity to understand their journey at a deeper level, and writing it down has been my privilege.

Finally, what follows are thoughts and insights – learnings I'll call them, for lack of a better word, about grief. Not from a clinical grief professional's or expert's perspective, but just from ours: seven siblings that experienced the traumatic death of a parent. There are five things we'd like to pass along after reflecting on our experiences. We hope these are helpful to you.

First, a person's life can be influenced by someone who dies maybe even more than by someone still living. Several of us measured many of our daily actions, big and little decisions over all these years, by what Mom would think of that – would it please her as she looked down on us? The What Would Jesus Do ("WWJD?") question became for some of us ("WWMT?") What Would Mom Think? If she had been here, she would have provided us with her guidance sometimes, but since she wasn't, we got to do the interpreting. We tried to honor what she'd wanted for us.

Second, life is short, so don't waste a day. Our lives may be short or long, we just don't know. Each day counts as it may be our last. Don't count on tomorrow to tell those you love that you do. Do it today. My siblings each expressed their realization of the importance of each day, each moment.

I still regret my words to Mom the last time I saw her, as they drove away to the hospital that fateful night in 1970. If I'd known it was the last time I'd ever see her, I'd have said, "Thank you for being such a good Mom," or a simple "I love you, Mom." But no, I said that stupid "tie up the score" quip. My last words to the person I loved so much were so shallow.

The third learning is about control, or really the lack thereof. After many years of contemplation on why we lost Mom, we each came to the realization that no one has control over life. We only control how we feel and act and react to what happens. We control whether to be happy or not. Whether to hate or not. Whether to work hard, with persistence and determination, or not. We can't control what happens, but we can control how we respond to what happens. Each of us learned this in different ways, through different struggles along our grief journey, but all felt it to be true.

Fourth, after much struggle, I do accept that faith will get you through anything, no matter how hard, if you open your heart to it. In whatever form that faith is to you. I believe my siblings would agree. Things happen that are beyond comprehension, questions can live without answers, and we will never know the Why of God's choice in taking our Mom. We feel we can choose to have faith, to believe in Him not in spite of, but because of this.

We know she's there watching over all of us. We seven siblings grew strong together, looked out for each other, and stayed a family. We hope that sharing our story gives you hope that you can make it through your grief journey and grow from the experience too.

I wish I had some of my siblings' levels of belief. Betty's absolute trust in His Plan. Tom's closure in seeing the billboard from God. Annie's long journey back to Jesus, fueled by belief in His grace and second chances. Bill's renewal from his anger. Dan's love for her even though he can't remember. Gary's trust in God's final accounting. I'll keep working on my faith.

They say the only things in life that are certain are death and taxes. I'd like to add another – and that is grief. Most of us aren't getting out of this world without losing someone we care about. No one escapes these feelings, so let's all help each other embrace them.

In this spirit, our fifth and final learning is that we need to do more to help others who are grieving, whether the griever is ourselves, someone we love or most importantly, our children.

In earlier generations, there were cultural norms about grieving. Grieving people wore black for a prescribed number of months, didn't participate in social events or work for a fixed period of time. Current norms tend to push grief under the rug, saying as so many did to us: "Get over it." Quickly! We're uncomfortable with your crying and carrying on: "Get over it." Get back to work or school and don't act like anything has changed.

Grief is ignored, hoping it will go away. People don't know what to say, so they ignore the bereaved or, worse yet, unintentionally say things that are hurtful. The very normal expressions of sadness should be encouraged as healthy grieving – and all of us can help change this norm.

I realize as I write this, chastising "us" as a society, that I myself have not done a very good job of helping others grieve. I attend visitations and funerals. I give memorials and send flowers or cards. I taught our children the importance of these simple acts. However, I don't always follow up and offer my support to those grieving in ways that can be impactful to their healing. I plan to do better.

If you are struggling with grief, open the door and let others in to help and care for you, especially those who have traveled this road in their past. When all those people at the visitation and funeral say, "Let me know if there's anything I can do," follow up and let them know how they can help.

If you or someone you love is struggling with grief, consider counseling or visit a local grief center or church grief group for help. Organizations like Heartlinks Grief Center, where I volunteer, can help you know that you are not alone in your grief journey. They can enable growth through your grief with individual and group counseling. Their help can improve communications within a family about grief, avoiding that feeling that we had of each being alone in the grief process.

If you care about someone who is grieving, take action. Go to the visitation or services. Send those cards and flowers. Give a memorial. Be like my teacher and just spend a moment hugging that child, or like Gary's friends and show up for the visitation. Be like my friend Nancy when I broke down in the high school hallway, and Tom's classmates who covered for him in reading class. Or like the cute boy in the high school hallway that made me cry. Even though I didn't respond well at the time, I knew he was trying to make me feel better, and I still treasure his kindness.

Pray for those grieving. So many people prayed for us, most of whom we didn't even know were praying. People in our little St. Libory community, the nuns at Ruma, family and friends and people we didn't know at all. Prayers are powerful gifts in the grieving process. Give them generously.

Talk with the person who is grieving and let them know you care. They will remember. There are usually lots of people around the first weeks, bringing food and comfort. Then, most people are left all alone with their grief. Be the one to call the person grieving in the weeks and months that follow the death and invite them for dinner or go visit with them.

Many of the seven of us have the painful memory of people in church or school staring or whispering about our family, but not talking to us. When you see people that have lost a loved one on the street or in church, go talk with them, not ignore them for fear of saying the wrong thing.

Just talk - about the weather or other simple topics. Just be there for them, letting them talk as much or as little as they need. Hugs help. Don't judge that they are "carrying on, crying too much, or being too sad." Be there for them. Have patience.

Sometimes just sitting quietly with them is the best thing to do and what they may need most.

We had a dear friend, Rosie, who lived across the street from us in Decatur, Illinois. It was our first move away from our home area, in 1988. She was a "character," outspoken and loud, but caring and loving too. The kind of character who would poke at your chest to make a point. She and her husband, Lambert, didn't have any children and they quickly became our adopted grandparents in Decatur. Joy and Ab loved them dearly.

When Lambert died unexpectedly in 1991 Rosie sank deeply into a sad, sad place. For months, years, she cried. I confess I lost patience with her, trying to cajole her out of her funk. I realize now, that was wrong. She just needed to grieve in her own way, in her own time. Our kids were much better with her, just spending time and talking with her.

Everyone grieves on their own timeline, has their own individual grief response and way of mourning. As someone wanting to help others grieve, it's important to honor their journey, not impose our own schedule or experience. What works for me may not for you, so seek to understand and then support, not edict what the griever needs to do.

Our Aunt Clara told me about her grief journey after her husband, Jim, died 35 years ago. She was coaxed into attending a "grief group" at her church by one of her dear friends. Her friend was certain the group sharing would help Aunt Clara heal as much as it had helped her after the death of her husband. For Aunt Clara, it was torture. She told me, "I felt grateful for my friend wanting to help. I went several times but each time I felt worse, not better. Talking about the pain made it worse for me. I realized I was coping well on my own, in my own way."

Dan's inability to remember Mom points to another important part of grief. Keep the deceased alive through talking about them, remembering them, honoring them. Memorials that are tangible, like our picnic bench for Mom, can help a grieving heart hold onto the memory of their lost loved one. Some families have started charitable organizations that raise funds for good causes to remember their loved ones that have died. There are a host of scholarships and memorial donations from which to choose in honor of lost loved ones, and they make the giving party feel better too. Taking action can give us a different kind of strength in our grief.

If you are a parent or caring adult helping a child deal with the loss of their parent, remember they simply cannot deal with the loss rationally. Inform them honestly about the death of their parent and listen to their concerns. Don't ignore that they are grieving too. Understand each child will grieve differently and act and react differently. All seven of us remember Mom's death and burial and the months afterwards differently, and each coped with our grief and mourned differently. From Gary's workaholic behavior, to Annie's overwhelming guilt, to my anger at Dad and God and incessant busyness, to Betty's rush to adulthood, to Bill's internalized rage, to Tom's rocking to Dan's wiping it all from his memory.

The seven of us siblings, while we had each other and tried to help each other through, could not be enough for one another. We each felt alone in our grief in the absence of Dad or some caring adult to help us cope. As adults, we typically have matured enough to know that death is part of life, part of the bargain in "dust to dust." As children, we were just not able to comprehend this yet. It's important to recognize that children – and teenagers are children too - need help, like they do with most things, to learn how to grieve.

Watch your children carefully; they may repress their grief and anger and need professional help to recover. Look for signs, such as grades falling or drastic changes in behavior or mood or friends. Get them to a local grief center or counseling center, or to your pastor or faith-based resource or retreat. They may say they don't want or need help, but these resources can make all the difference in their grief journey and life, as religious retreats and counseling ultimately did for many of us. Maybe our family would not have lost our beautiful Annie for a decade, and the family's first grandchild if someone had intervened.

I've included a short list of resources on grief, both organizations and on-line resources, in Appendix B, and there are many others available. There are many excellent books on grief and helping others cope with grief. I've included a list of both Heartlinks Grief Center's favorite books and some of mine in Appendix C.

So many of you, dear readers, have traveled or are traveling a difficult grief journey. Our hope is that these learnings and resources will help you and those you love in your grief and your life. My husband Bill and I have a good friend and neighbor, Dorothy Borrenpohl, who is 92. She knows grief. She lost her mother at 15, and her husband at 48. Her faith has seen her through. She told me recently, "Believe in Jesus, put your trust in Him. Count your blessings and they will outnumber the hard, grief-filled times."

WWMT (What Would Mom Think)? We lost her, but I think Mom would agree.

Appendix A

Sibling Interview Questionnaire

Name: _____

1. What are your favorite memories of Mom from before her death?

2. Are there any family stories that you would like to be sure are included?

3. Who told you Mom had died?

4. What was your first reaction?

5. Do you remember what happened that first day after she died, before the visitation night? What did you do?

6. Do you remember what the adults said about Mom's death?

7. What do you recall about the funeral and the arrangements in the next few days?

8. What were your last words to her? Last interaction?

9. Going back to school – what do you remember about it?

10. Life at home was changed, describe how it was for you?

11. Did you cry, or how did you express your grief?

12. What do you remember about the next few weeks? Specific details of things that happened?

13. How did you feel about Dad after Mom's death?

14. Do you remember who came to the house and helped? And who didn't?

15. What got you through those first days without Mom?

16. After she died, who do you remember was kind or helpful to you?

17. What do you remember changed in our daily routine as a family after she died?

18. Do you remember our first Christmas without her?

19. Other holidays and special days that you recalled in the first year?

20. What took your mind off the pain of her being gone? How did you cope?

21. Did you talk with anyone about how you felt, your grief?

22. Did her death change your relationship with anyone?

23. Did her death alter how you thought about God?

24. Did your friends understand what you were going through? Express it?

25. How did you deal with any anger you had about losing her?

26. What ways did your grief carry into your adult life?

27. How did her death change your life?

28. Do you think your life would have been very different had she lived? How?

29. Have you felt her presence in your life? How and when?

30. When have you most missed her?

31. Did you do things in your life that were "in her name," that you knew would have made her proud/happy with you?

32. What do you think she would say if she were here today about you and your life?

33. If you could go back and say anything to her, what would it be?

34. Do you have any special memories of Dad's illness, death and funeral you'd like to share?

35. What else?

Appendix B

Resources for Grievers

A small sampling of organizations and resources that can provide assistance with a grief journey. There are many others but I am hopeful these can get you started.

Organization/ Resource name	Website	Description
Heartlinks Grief Center	http://myheartlinks.com/	Provides grief services to all in Southwestern Illinois
National Alliance for Grieving Children	https://childrengrieve.org/	National association that supports grieving children and organizations that aid them
The Dougy Center	https://www.dougy.org/	The first national children's grief center and a leader in the field for grieving children and families

Centering Corporation	http://www.centering.org/	Grief books and resources
Compassion Books	http://www.compassion-books.com/	Grief books and resources
Grief Watch	https://www.griefwatch.com/support-group	Grief books and resources
Hello Grief	http://www.hellogrief.org/	Online resources to share about grief and loss, listing of resources by state
Share Grief	http://www.sharegrief.com/	Online grief support, education and resources
WHAT'S YOUR GRIEF?	https://whatsyourgrief.com/	Online weekly blog and articles about your grief journey
KIDSAID	http://www.kidsaid.com/	Kids email support group
Grief Net	http://www.griefnet.org/	Internet community of people dealing with grief

Appendix C

A Helpful Reading List

Below are some recommended books on grief which Heartlinks Grief Center finds helpful with grievers along their journey. Also included are some of my favorites.

I Wasn't Ready to Say Goodbye
Brook Noel and Pamela D. Blair, PH.D.; Sourcebooks, Inc., 2000

Tender Fingerprints
Brad Stetson; Zondervan, 1999

Parenting Through Crisis: Helping Kids in Times of Loss, Grief, And Change.
Barbara Coloroso; Harper Collins Publishing, 2001

Helping Children Live with Death and Loss
Dianah Seibert, Judy C. Drolet, Joyce V. Fetro; SIUE Press, 2001

When Children Grieve: For Adults to Help Children Deal with Death, Divorce, Pet Loss, Moving, and Other Losses
James, John W; Friedman, Russell; Harper Collins Publishing, 2001

In The Presence Of Grief: Helping Family Members Resolve Death, Dying and Bereavement Issues
Dorothy S. Becvar; The Guilford Press, 2001

Helping Bereaved Children: A Handbook for Practitioners
Nancy Boyd Weber, Editor; The Guilford Press, 2010

A Grace Disguised
Jerry Sittser; Zondervan, 1995

Soul Healing: A Spiritual Orientation in Counseling and Healing
Dorothy S. Becvar; Basic Books, 1997

Understanding Your Grief: Ten Essential Touchstones for Finding Hope and Healing Your Heart
Allen D Wolfelt, Ph.D.;Companion Press, 2003

I'm Grieving As Fast I Can: How young Widows and Widowers Can Cope and Heal
Linda Feinberg; New Horizon Press, 1994

Help for the Hard Times: Getting Through Loss
Earl Hipp; Hazelden, 1995 (This book is specifically for teens)

Author Biography

Ellen Krohne
September 2017

Ellen Krohne has been blessed to have had many "acts" in her work life. She's worked as a utility employee, from front-line customer service to an executive, as an international business consultant, as executive director of a not-for-profit organization, and she has her own consulting practice, Yellow Energy Consulting. She treasures her bachelor's and master's degrees in organizational management, both earned as an adult while working full time and raising a family.

Ellen is currently enjoying being a grandparent and doing lots of volunteer work in retirement with her husband, Bill. She feels grateful to have authored her first book, *We Lost Her*, and to have learned so much about

Ellen Krohne

grief, faith and her family in the process. She is looking forward to a writing career as her "next act."

"You Can if You Think You Can"